Foreword

Since its establishment in 2002, the Mental Health Commission has advocated the involvement of service users in all aspects of the mental health services, ranging from involvement in individual care and treatment plans to involvement in service planning and delivery. Ascertaining and responding to the views of service users in relation to the mental health care system is fundamental to promoting service user involvement.

In recent years, a number of consultative processes have been undertaken with service users, carers, service providers and planners on their current assessment of mental health services in Ireland and their recommendations for future models of mental health care. These include the consultation undertaken by the Expert Group on Mental Health Policy published in 2004[1][2] and the report on stakeholder consultation on quality in mental health services published by the Mental Health Commission in 2005[3].

The Mental Health Commission, in 2003, decided to commission a study of the views of adult mental health service users on the organisational aspects of publicly funded mental health services. Dr. Elizabeth A. Dunne, Department of Applied Psychology, University College Cork was engaged to conduct the study on behalf of the Mental Health Commission. There are two parts to the study – part one involves focus groups with service user peer support groups and a carer group; part two involves face-to-face interviews with persons who are not active members of user representative groups (known as independents in this study). The Mental Health Commission, in particular, wished to hear the views of those who may not have had the opportunity to express their views previously. Key themes from the study refer to the therapeutic relationship and contact with therapists, giving and sharing information and models of service provision.

A clear vision has now emerged from recent publications on mental health services in Ireland on how the services should be structured and delivered. Implementing this new model with its emphasis on multidisciplinary, community-based, recovery orientated interventions will lead to a model of service delivery greatly different to that experienced by the service users in this study. However, it will be important to continue to conduct research on these innovative practices in mental health service delivery to ensure that the services are in line with best practice and of a high standard.

---

1   Expert Group on Mental Health Policy (2004a) Speaking Your Mind : A Report on the Public Consultation Process, Department of Health and Children.

2   Expert Group on Mental Health Policy (2004b) What We Have Heard : A Report on the Service User Consultation Process, Department of Health and Children.

3   Mental Health Commission (2005a), Quality in Mental Health – Your Views, A Report on Stakeholder Consultation on Quality in Mental Health Services, Dublin : Mental Health Commission.

Last year the Mental Health Commission published its research strategy[4] with the explicit purpose of enhancing mental health services research capacity in Ireland. To date the body of research on mental health services in Ireland is limited and its impact on shaping policy and service delivery has been minimal. The Mental Health Commission is committed to promoting an evidence-based approach to the delivery of mental health services. This research study adds to the body of knowledge on how mental health services are delivered in Ireland.

The Mental Health Commission wishes to thank Dr. Dunne and her colleagues for all their work and commitment to this research study. We wish to thank the service user organisations and personnel in the Health Service Executive for their input, assistance and support. But above all else, we wish to thank all those who participated in the study. This study would not have been possible without their agreement to participate, and their willingness to share their views and ideas with all of us.

Bríd Clarke
Chief Executive Officer

July 2006

---

4   *Mental Health Commission (2005b), Research Strategy.*

Acknowledgments

Sincere thanks are due to the following persons, groups, and organisations who facilitated this research project:-

The 85 service users and carers who took part in either the focus groups or the 'Independent' interviews, and the 4 people who wrote to us about their experience and suggestions.

The National Executives/Boards and the local coordinators of AWARE; Bodywhys; GROW; Irish Advocacy Network; Out-and-About; RECOVERY (Ireland) Inc.; and Schizophrenia Ireland (Lucia Foundation) who facilitated the focus groups. Ms. Noreen Fitzgibbon, Mr. Donal Geaney, Ms. Barbara O'Callaghan, Mr. Robert O'Connell, Ms. Jenny O'Reilly, Ms. Mags Ryan, and Ms. Margaret Trafford were especially helpful to us.

The Clinical Directors and Consultant Psychiatrists who supported the principle of the project taking place at their units, and the Mental Health Service programme managers and their deputies at the (former) North-Western Health Board, the South-West Area Health Board, the Southern Health Board who put us in touch with our liaison persons.

Our liaison persons with the mental health service division of the participating services, Dr. John Wallace at Letterkenny General Hospital and Drs. O'Flynn and Mulligan at Sligo General Hospital; Mr. Oliver Claffey at the Jonathan Swift Clinic; Mr. Michael Looney at St. Stephen's Hospital, Ms. Mary Keohane at Mercy University Hospital, Mr. Michael Cotterell, Mr. John Linehan and Ms. Jean Landers at Cork University Hospital, Ms. Helen Ahern at Ravenscourt, and Ms. Frankie Moynihan at Tus Nua, and Mr. Ned Brosnan at Tralee General Hospital, were especially helpful to us.

Ms. Mette Jensen-Kavanagh, Ms. Margaret Cahill (St. James' Hospital) and Dr. Carmel O'Sullivan, who piloted our application through the various Ethics Committees.

The sub-group of the *Mental Health Commission*, Ms. Brid Clarke CEO, Mr. Diarmuid Ring and Mr. Mike Watts (Commission), who liaised with us on behalf of the *Commission* and who facilitated contacts and – with Dr. Fiona Keogh, Research Consultant to the Commission – advised on the final draft of the report. Notwithstanding their guidance, responsibility for the report and the views expressed lies with the writer.

Glossary and Other Explanatory Notes

CPN –   Community Psychiatric Nurse also known as CMHN or Community Mental Health Nurse

DAY HOSPITAL –   A facility designed to 'provide intensive treatment equivalent to that available in a hospital inpatient setting for acutely ill' persons. (Hickey, Moran and Walsh, 2003, p.18).

DAY CENTRE –   'The role of the psychiatric day centre is to provide social care for patients…Both day centres and day hospitals have a therapeutic role but unlike day hospitals, the orientation of day centres is social' (Hickey, Moran and Walsh, 2003, p.18).

GP –   General Practitioner

Health Boards -   Prior to January 2005 the health services in Ireland were administered as regional units covering specific geographic areas and were known as 'Health Boards'. These Boards had a level of autonomy in the disbursement of the funds given to them. Since January 2005, the Heath Service Executive assumed the responsibility for the delivery of health services.

ICD –   International Classification of Diseases

NCHD –   Non-consultant Hospital Doctors (previously known as 'Junior Doctors').

Sectioned Admission –   Now called an *involuntary admission.* This term has been used in the past and is still sometimes used to refer to a situation where the service user is admitted to inpatient care against his/her will. This requires medical sanction before it can be done.

SHO –   Senior House Officer. A term used to refer to a grade within the NCHD category.

Service User –   People who experience or have experienced mental illness and accessed mental health services.

Research Team

Principal Investigator	Dr. Elizabeth Dunne Ph.D
Moderators of the Focus Groups	Dr. John McCarthy Ph.D.
	Aine Fitzpatrick, M.Sc.
Co-Moderators	Dr. Paul Sullivan Ph.D.
	Jacqueline Henry, B.A.
	Jennifer O'Mahony-Yeager, M.Phil.
Interviewers	Martina O'Riordan, M.Sc.
	Tina Powell, B.Soc.Sc.
	David Shannon, M.Sc.
Research Assistant Phase 1	Jacqueline Henry, B.A.
Research Assistant Phase 2 (July – October, 2004)	Maria Delaney, B.A.
Research Assistant Phase 2 (November 2004 - April 2005)	David Shannon, M.Sc.

Principal Investigator's Preface

In the course of this project the researchers were privileged to meet with and hear the views of service users, carers, and those mental health professionals who liaised with us in organising Phase 2 of the project. We were greatly impressed by the dedication of the professionals and by the desire of service users and carers to work with all those involved in service provision and delivery to ensure a caring and effective mental health service in this country.

It would be a disservice to those who took part in the research project if this report was to be read as a catalogue of complaints and criticism and not as a blueprint for development. Participants identified either directly or by implication the kind of changes that once implemented will make a significant difference to their efforts to cope with the psychological and psychiatric difficulties they face. As discussed in the final section of this report, many of these changes do not have a financial cost but depend upon the good-will and creativity of individuals and organisations in modifying the way in which their service is delivered to users and carers.

With our participants we hope that this report will be thoughtfully read in a spirit of open-mindedness and a willingness to learn from those who can provide a unique view based on personal experience.

E.A. Dunne
Deptartment of Applied Psychology, U.C.C.

Cork, 2005

Part 1

PART ONE

Part 1

Introduction to the Project

Preamble to Part 1 and Report Overview

Background to the Project

Persons who use the mental health services are key stakeholders within the health system, and their situation and concerns are the focus of the Mental Health Act 2001. Arising from the remit given it in that Act, the Mental Health Commission wished to document adult users' views of the mental health services they have received, and to identify ways in which the mental health services could be developed to better meet their needs. The mental health services have a varied client base. For example, they aim to serve adults, persons with special learning needs and mental health difficulties, older adults, children and adolescents, people with problems relating to addictive behaviours of many kinds, and people with forensic needs. This list is not exhaustive. The focusing of this project on adult users of the service is not in any way intended to imply that the Mental Health Commission does not appreciate the needs of other groups.

Approach to Data Collection and Analysis

The research focus was on the organisational aspects of the publicly funded mental health service. While participants themselves often referred to the psychological events that had led them to use the services, this project is not about participants' psychological and psychiatric states as such. Rather the focus is on their experience of the service they receive when they seek assistance from the mental health services funded by the state. Based on the views expressed, observations on the services and possible strategic actions are put forward for consideration and response by the Mental Health Commission.

Chronology

Following meetings between the CEO of the Commission and two Commission members and a member of the Department of Applied Psychology, U.C.C on May 21st and August 7th 2003, and the review of a preliminary and then a final proposal by the Commission, the Department was contracted to carry out a study of users' views.

The initial proposal was for a 10-month project with two phases. Although the phases could have been carried out in tandem, this proved impractical for a variety of reasons mentioned below. Consequently Phase 1, which involved focus group meetings with eight user mutual help organisations, began in November 2003 and was completed (including participant sign-off) by May 2004. Phase 2 involved individual interviews with persons currently using the mental health services who were not active members of any representative group at the time of the study. Phase 2 commenced in August 2004 and was completed by January 2005. Data collection for this phase took 5 months longer than anticipated, reflecting such factors as the changes in the Health Board system which were pending throughout the project, receiving approval from the ethics committees of the various boards and in some cases individual service facilities, and arranging appointments which would cause the least disruption possible to participants[1].

Report Format

There are 3 parts to this report. Part 1 which includes this Introduction and Overview, describes the research method used and discusses the technical issues associated with it. Part 2 presents the findings under each of the topic headings used to orientate the focus group discussions and the interviews with individual service users. Part 3 reviews the findings and raises matters which need to be considered by those involved in delivering a quality service to the users of the publicly funded mental health services.

A numbering sequence for parts, sections, and paragraphs within sections is used in Parts 1 and 3 to help readers to locate material they may wish to consult. Thus the sequence 1.1.1 refers to Section 1 (on Choice of Research Method) and to paragraph 1 sub-paragraph 1 within that section.

The format used in Sections 4, 5, and 7 in Part 2 follows the topics used to guide the group discussions and the individual interviews and includes supporting verbatim extracts from participants. The focus groups summaries from which these illustrative quotes were taken are given in Appendix IV. This format was chosen so that as far as possible readers could hear the voices of the participants with the minimum of interference from the writer's professional filter.

---

[1]   The possibility of this kind of delay was signalled to the Commission at the outset.

PART ONE

Section 1

Choice of the Research Method

Section 1
Choice of the Research Method

1.0.0   Relevant Factors

1.1.0   The following factors guided the choice of research method:

- The purpose of the project

- The need to allow the reality of service users' experience of using the publicly funded mental health service to be expressed

- Ethical issues

- Sampling issues

1.2.0   Since the purpose of the project was to obtain the views of users' on the service available to them, a survey was the obvious method of choice.

1.3.0   Focus groups and the semi-structured narrative interview were used to ensure that service users' experience when availing of services, and their views on how the services might be further developed were recorded. Both approaches are widely used in qualitative research in the psychological and social sciences.

1.3.1   These methods and the qualitative analysis of the findings obtained allow people to describe their experiences and to express their views on them using topic headings relevant to the research question. The topic headings are supplied by the researcher to keep the account focused on the issue being investigated, but unlike structured questionnaires or interviews, respondents are not required to use pre-determined response categories. Thus participants can focus the research on the issues that are important to them within the usually quite generous boundaries of the topic headings.

1.3.2   Qualitative analysis has the added advantage of not only identifying the aspects of a service that users find of more or less benefit to them, it also allows respondents to say what about a particular aspect of service makes it so. Thus the service provider can know more precisely the elements of their service that need to be modified and in what way. The elements that should be retained are also clearly identified.

1.4.0   The following considerations were relevant to the ethical aspect of this project.

- A person experiencing an acute episode of anxiety or disordered thinking would probably not be able to engage in conversation with the interviewer or to contribute to a group discussion at all or without undue distress.

○ It might also be the case that a person who is psychologically able to tell their story in the cognitive sense may not feel emotionally well enough to do so. For example, it may be upsetting for someone to review their situation if sad or unpleasant experiences are recalled.

○ A service user might become concerned if approached to participate because they fear that it means they are more unwell than they believed.

○ Members of an organisation or individual users of services may fear that confidentiality had been breached if they are approached to participate without sufficient prior consultation and explanation of what the project is about by trusted others.

○ Someone who really does not want to participate may feel obliged to do so because of being approached in a formal and official way. Thus they may comply against their own better judgement.

1.4.1   With these and other similar possibilities in mind, we decided that potential participants would be approached by the national executives in the case of the service user organisations, and by the mental health professionals personally known to individual service users. We judged that the professionals and the local group co-ordinators would know how well someone was; whether they would be upset by talking about their experiences; and/or whether they might be inclined to give consent in order to be helpful or to comply with authority. Thus they could safeguard would-be participants.

1.4.2   The decisions made on the ethical issues impacted on the approach taken to sampling the population of service users. The requirements for random sampling could not be met since the ethical issues described above meant that not all service users had an equal chance of being selected for the survey[2].

Random sampling was also not appropriate in the case of the user organisations since many of these keep no record of membership, people being free to attend meetings as they need to. It would also be against the philosophy of many of the groups to appear to depersonalise the members by selecting them through randomisation rather than by asking for volunteers. Given these factors maximum variation sampling of service users from 3 former Health Board areas and a volunteer sample of members of user organisations who agreed to take part were the sampling procedures followed. Sampling will be discussed further in Section 2.

---

2   *In fact in the absence of an IT system for patient records in all of the mental health services, the compilation of a random sample would have put a well nigh impossible demand on the administrative staffs of the service units within the (former) Health Boards.*

Section 2

Developing the Research Design and Method

Section 2

Developing the Research Design and Method

2.1.0 Research Design

2.1.1 The survey of service users' views was carried out in two phases. **Phase 1** consisted of focus group meetings with representatives of the following service user mutual help organisations: *AWARE; GROW; RECOVERY Inc.; Schizophrenia Ireland; Bodywhys; Out-and-About;* and *Irish Advocacy Network*. An eighth group consisting of *Carers* from *Schizophrenia Ireland's* carer support section also took part. A ninth organisation was invited, but declined to participate since it was undertaking a development programme that required its full attention at the time. **Phase 2** involved individual face-to-face interviews with persons who were not active members of a user representative group at the time of the study. Some were inpatients and others were attending outpatients, day centres, or day hospitals run by their local mental health service. These persons were called 'Independents' for the purposes of this study.

2.1.2 The method of data collection was similar in both phases. Each involved participants giving an account of their experiences of using the state-funded mental health service, identifying the aspects of the services that they found most useful, and suggesting areas where improvement could be made. The topics used to guide the focus groups and individual interviews are given in Appendix III. The suitability of the wording and the feasibility of using the interview method with 'Independent' service users were checked in a pilot study. It will be clear from Appendix III that the difference between Phases 1 and 2 lies more in the setting in which the information was collected (group vs. individual one-to-one) than in the format through which it was elicited.

2.1.3 Two persons who had been involved in caring for service users became aware of the project and contacted the researcher directly to express their views. This information is not directly referred to in this report but it did inform the research in a general way. Twenty-four people who were experiencing eating distress and became aware of the project through the cooperation of *Bodywhys*[3,4] made their views known to the researcher. These contributions are drawn on in Sections 5 and Section 6.

2.2.0 Ethical Approval

The design, method, and procedure of the project were developed according to the Code of Ethics of the Psychological Society of Ireland. The written proposal was then submitted for review by a senior member of the staff of the Department of Applied Psychology who was not involved with the project.

---

3   *Bodywhys made the interview format available on their website and these independent respondents contacted the project by giving their views in written form following the topic headings, and e-mailing this to the Principal Investigator.*

4   *The Marino Therapy Centre became aware of the project through the Bodywhys web site and circulated copies of the form to members. The information obtained was used in Sections 4 and 5 as appropriate. A fuller analysis of these data will be carried out and made available to the Commission in due course.*

The project proposal was then submitted to the ethics committees of each of the participating former Health Boards/Hospitals and/or to their mental health service facilities where this was required as part of established practice within a Board.

Clarification of various points was given where requested and approval was eventually received from all three Boards/Hospitals.

2.3.0   Recruitment Procedure

2.3.1   The participants in the focus groups volunteered to take part. They were approached on behalf of the project by their national executive and/or local co-ordinators who had been supplied with full details of the research which they could pass on to would-be participants. The request was for seven persons to take part in each group but fewer or more than this number could be accommodated. Where the group was composed of 7 – 10 persons, we asked that not more than three should be former users of the services. Where the group was 4 - 6 persons we asked that not more than two should be former service users. With the exception of the *Carer* group all participants were to have had direct personal experience of the publicly funded mental health service. Persons with experience of private services were not excluded, but the focus would be on their experience of the state funded service.

2.3.2   Thirty-seven people took part in the focus groups. The mean number of participants was 5 and the range was from 3 – 7. Seventy-eight percent of the focus group participants (excluding the *Carer* group) were current service users.

2.3.3   Individual interviewees (Independents) were recruited through the three (former) Health Boards who agreed to take part in the project when approached by the Mental Health Commission to do so. The participating Boards were chosen on the basis of the nature of their catchments. Thus the former North Western Health Board had a strong rural dimension to its catchment; the former South-West Area Health Board, serving south inner-city Dublin and Co. Kildare at the time of the project had a mainly urban clientele; and the former Southern Health Board had a mixed urban and rural population base.

2.3.4   Each of the participating areas appointed a member of the nursing, or of the consultant or non-consultant medical staff to liaise with members of the project team in inviting service users to take part, arranging for them to give their consent, and arranging appointments with an interviewer. The liaison persons based their decision to approach a would-be participant on the ethical considerations set out in paragraph 1.4.0 in the previous section and on profile criteria (see Table 2.1) used to operationally define the variables relevant to maximum variation sampling for this project.

2.4.0 Validity of the Sampling Methods

2.4.1 As already noted the members of the focus groups were volunteers. Except in research where data relevant to the topic of interest are obtained as a 'by-product' as it were of a procedure that the participant has already agreed to or of an activity in which s/he is naturally engaged[5], all samples have a volunteer element. Even when selected through the statistical process of randomisation, people may give or with hold their consent when asked to take part in a research project.

2.4.2 Not withstanding this, volunteer samples are frequently criticised because of fears that persons who volunteer may not be typical of the population in which one is interested. It could be argued that service users who volunteered for this project might have particularly positive or negative views of the service they had received; might have had a-typical experiences because of where they received the service; or might have been or be more or less well than service users usually are.

2.4.3 There are 4 reasons to be confident that the volunteers in this project give a valid picture of the typical experience of the users of the publicly funded mental health service.

○ The verbatim accounts of volunteers' experiences (Appendix IV) are balanced rather than biased in either a positive or negative direction.

○ The moderators and co-moderators noted the absence of bias on the part of contributors and their manifest wish to give a fair but realistic account of their experiences.

○ There is nothing to support a view that participants' experiences can be attributed to provider-specific factors. The participants in the different groups came from a variety of geographical locations and many had had experience of more than one mental health service provider within Ireland.

○ Most participants spontaneously stated at some stage during the group meeting that they were participating because they *"wanted to help make the service better for others – for all of us"; "hoped something would happen with [was happening at last; would finally be done about] the mental health services."* Clearly the motivation of these participants to take part in the project was to be constructive and to contribute to service development.

---

5 *For example if the researcher is interested in the kinds of music bought by customers of music stores in different locations in a city the data can be obtained by examining the store's stock records. Nobody is required to buy an item or a particular item so there is no risk of infringement of rights or of putting someone at risk.*

2.4.4 On the more general point that the views of persons who join mental health user groups may differ significantly from those who do not join, Crawford and Rutter (2004) note that there is no evidence to support such a position. They consider that both cohorts have similar concerns.

2.4.5 'Independent' participants were selected using 'maximum variation sampling' (MVS), to achieve full coverage of the range of user experiences and views while allowing in depth discussion of their experience. MVS deliberately includes persons who represent the extremes of the variables (i.e. factors relevant to the research) that persons with knowledge of the area under investigation consider critical. The reasoning underlying this approach to sampling is that by including people who are very different from each other in terms of their exposure to the variables that are crucial to the investigation, their accounts will cover the full spectrum of what is experienced by the whole of the population in which the researcher is interested, (Know Your Audience)[6]. In this project the population of mental health service users would be represented by the persons with the combinations of psychological events and patterns of service use set out in the profiles discussed next.

2.4.6 A number of relevant variables were identified by the researchers and the members of the sub-group from the Commission involved with this project. The practicability of using these variables to identify possible participants was then discussed at a meeting with the mental health Programme Managers of the participating Boards. It emerged that it would not be possible to use the criteria of the Central Statistics office to select for urban vs. rural domicile since such precise information on population density in a given area would not be known to mental health personnel. It would also be difficult to achieve diversity among those service users likely to be living in hostel accommodation since such accommodation is in short supply.

2.4.7 The final set of variables used in the maximum variation sample were:

○ Gender (male or female) of the participant.

○ Age of participant (18-30 years; 30+ years)

○ Nature of psychological/psychiatric problem as defined by the International Classification of Diseases (ICD).

○ Duration of experience of the publicly funded mental health service (under or over 3 years).

---

6   *This website which is referenced in the Bibliography, gives a very clear and easy-to-follow discussion of issues involved in sampling.*

2.4.8 The 32 profiles set out in Table 2.1 is the template used to assemble the maximum variation sample of Independent participants. For example, Profile 1 is for a man, experiencing schizophrenia as defined by the ICD code for this category, who has been using mainstream mental health services for less than 3 years, and who is aged 18-30 years.

Table 2.1 Profiles of 'Independents' Sought from Each of 3 Health Boards

Profile	Gender	Age	Duration	Schizophrenia	Depression	Bipolar	Anxiety
1	Male	18-30	<3yrs.	*			
2	Male	18-30	<3yrs.		*		
3	Male	18-30	<3yrs.			*	
4	Male	18-30	<3yrs.				*
5	Male	30+	<3yrs.	*			
6	Male	30+	<3yrs.		*		
7	Male	30+	<3yrs.			*	
8	Male	30+	<3yrs.				*
9	Male	18-30	>3yrs.	*			
10	Male	18-30	>3yrs.		*		
11	Male	18-30	>3yrs.			*	
12	Male	18-30	>3yrs.				*
13	Male	30+	>3yrs.	*			
14	Male	30+	>3yrs.		*		
15	Male	30+	>3yrs.			*	
16	Male	30+	>3yrs.				*
17	Female	18-30	<3yrs.	*			
18	Female	18-30	<3yrs.		*		
19	Female	18-30	<3yrs.			*	
20	Female	18-30	<3yrs.				*
21	Female	30+	<3yrs.	*			
22	Female	30+	<3yrs.		*		
23	Female	30+	<3yrs.			*	
24	Female	30+	<3yrs.				*
25	Female	18-30	>3yrs.	*			
26	Female	18-30	>3yrs.		*		
27	Female	18-30	>3yrs.			*	
28	Female	18-30	>3yrs.				*
29	Female	30+	>3yrs.	*			
30	Female	30+	>3yrs.		*		
31	Female	30+	>3yrs.			*	
32	Female	30+	>3yrs.				*

2.4.9 The aim was to interview one person fulfiling each set of inclusion criteria from each of the participating Health Boards. This would mean three participants fulfiling the criteria for Profile 1 in the example just given. A total sample of 96 individual service users was sought. The sample achieved was 48 persons (50%). The profiles achieved over the three participating Boards are given in Table 2.2.

Table 2.2 'Independent' Profiles Achieved over 3 Health Boards

Profile	Gender	Age	Duration	Schizophrenia	Depression	Bipolar	Neuroses
1	Male	18-30yrs.	<3yrs.	**	*	*	*
2	Male	30+yrs.	<3yrs.	*	***		**
3	Male	18-30yrs.	>3yrs.	*	*	*	
4	Male	30+yrs.	>3yrs.	***	***	***	*
5	Female	18-30yrs.	<3yrs.				**
6	Female	30+yrs.	<3yrs.	*****	**	******	**
7	Female	18-30yrs.	>3yrs.	*	*	**	
8	Female	30+yrs.	>3yrs.	*	*	*	
ICD Category Totals				**14**	**12**	**14**	**8**

2.4.10 There were three reasons for not achieving the planned sample size.

○ Two facilities in one Health Board area were unable to take part within a time span that would allow this report to be produced without excessive further delay. This reduced the number of potential participants by 22 persons[7].

○ The participating facilities were not always able to find a person who would represent a particular profile and who was willing to take part in an interview[8].

○ Eleven interviewees did not turn up to the appointment with the interviewer and gave no reason for this[9],[10]. Three persons 'phoned to say they would not be taking part because something urgent had come up (1 person); or because of their own or a family member's physical illness (2 people). They were not in a position to schedule another appointment.

2.4.11 The following points can be made with regard to the effects of these factors on the validity of the findings from Phase 2.

---

7   *Since other facilities had difficulty in filling their quota, we considered it unreasonable to ask them to make up the short fall.*

8   *This was so for Profile 4, 7, 18, 20, 21 and 32 in two locations.*

9   *On the basis of 1 person who did not feel well on the day of the interview, but who made and kept an appointment for another day, it may be that those who did not keep their appointments did not feel up to talking on the appointed day and felt unable to make an alternative arrangement.*

10 *We do not have information on the profiles of these persons, since we received information on this only when a participant arrived for interview.*

O The situation of service users in the two non-participating facilities is better or worse than those pertaining to the facilities that took part. We have no means of assessing this, but we argue that either way because of the qualitative method of analysis used, their input could not have dominated the general trend in the narratives obtained since they would simply have been noted as describing predominantly positive or negative experiences of the service.

O The absence of representatives of some profiles from the sample of some facilities may be due to the seasonal variation in some conditions[11].

O Non-participation may have been due to a change of mind; to not feeling well on the day of the interview; or to problems with transport in getting to the interview. Again we have no means of knowing whether the experience of non-participants was more or less positive than that of those who participated, but – as suggested earlier – the use of qualitative analysis means that either extreme would not have overwhelmed the general trend emerging from the narratives.

2.4.12   Two other points must be considered concerning the validity of the sample of 'Independents'. These are:

O The effect of having mental health professionals choosing whom to invite to take part in the project.

O The motivation of individual participants.

2.4.13   We have no reason to believe that the mental health professionals who co-operated with us on this project were motivated by anything other than the best interests of their service users. In our discussions with them regarding the selection process they were as keen as the service users themselves to advance the quality of the service they were giving. The range of views obtained from the interviewees (which can be assessed by reading the material in Part 2 of this Report and in Appendix IV) confirmed the unbiased nature of the selection process carried out by the mental health professionals.

2.4.14   As with the participants in the focus groups the Independent participants were motivated to contribute to the development of the mental health care system. This is evident from their balanced and fair comments on various aspects of the services.

2.4.15   The validity of data obtained through qualitative analysis is established through the process of triangulation. This is further explained in Appendix V.

---

11   *We were informed that persons with mood swings made more use of the service in early summer, for example.*

Section 3

Data Collection and Analysis

Section 3
Data Collection and Analysis

3.1.0   Data Collection for Phase 1 - Focus Groups

3.1.1   Focus groups participants were fully informed about the purpose and nature of the research prior to their deciding to volunteer (see Appendix I). A person's presence throughout the group session was taken as indicating that s/he consented to being part of the project.

3.1.2   Participants were reminded at the outset of the meeting that we would like to tape the session to ensure accuracy and were asked whether they were all still agreeable to this. Permission to tape was given by all groups.

3.1.3   The moderator and co-moderator introduced themselves and participants did likewise, usually giving just their first name. Some participants were already known to each other through activities of the organisation that had facilitated the project. No record of names was kept by the researchers since verbatim extracts used in the report would not be attributed to individuals.

3.1.4   The average number of persons taking part in the groups was 5 with a range of from 3 – 7 participants. While 3 is below the recommended minimum, based on experience with this method of data collection the information from the smallest group was included because of the wealth of reflection and insight of the participants.

3.1.5   Each meeting was scheduled for 2$_{1/2}$ hours, allowing 2 hours for discussion with a 15 minute break for refreshment. In fact, although the moderator and co-moderator notified participants when the time for wrapping up the discussion was approaching, in all cases the participants themselves chose to run moderately over time (unless they had to catch a bus or car ride).

3.1.6   Each group's deliberations were kept on track by the moderator using the Discussion Guide. This is given in Appendix III. The co-moderator looked after the recording of the data; noted and made notes on the group's 'emotional tone'; and offered comments and short summaries as required.

3.1.7   As part of the data collection, the co-moderator asked participants to rank their key concerns and to rate each for its urgency/level of significance for service users before the conclusion of the group. The intention was that these data would allow a statement to be made about the generality and strength of the particular concerns expressed. It was evident after the first two groups that ranking was not practicable since a majority of participants in each group felt the items listed were really of equal importance to their service experience. Accordingly this part of data collection was discontinued and main concerns were simply listed.

3.1.8   The importance of the moderator and co-moderator being alert to the needs of participants and ensuring that they were not over-stressed by the process and had transport home were discussed by the research team in preparatory meetings. The 'Guidelines for Focus Group Moderators/Co-Moderators' is given in Appendix III.

3.2.0   Data Collection for Phase 2 - Interviews with 'Independents'

3.2.1   Each participant was interviewed in a suitably private setting with which the interviewee was familiar. This was generally a consulting room in an outpatient clinic, day centre, or day hospital, or in an inpatient facility. Two people who had transportation problems were interviewed in their own home.

3.2.2   Appointments were scheduled to last 45 minutes, allowing approximately 30 minutes for the interview and 15 minutes for explaining the purpose of the interview, answering participants' queries and 'winding down'.

3.2.3   As noted in the previous chapter, the topics covered in the 'Independent' interviews were the same as those in the focus group 'Discussion Guide', (Appendix III).

3.2.4   The material sent to the liaison person at each Board for circulation to would-be participants is given in Appendix I. This set of material included a 'Consent Form' (Appendix II) which Boards used if they wished[12]. The interviewers aimed to create an atmosphere where participants would feel free to stop the interview if they found it too demanding and/or could say if they did not wish their verbatim statements to be used in the report.

3.2.5   As in the case of the focus groups, all interviewers were alert to the possibility of interviewees becoming stressed or tired since they were the sole focus of the interview, as well as to ensuring that they had transport home. The 'Guideline for Interviewers' is given in Appendix III.

12   *Some Boards preferred to use forms designed by their own ethics committees.*

3.3.0   Data Analysis

3.3.1   The focus group tapes were transcribed verbatim. The views expressed in response to each Discussion Guide question were collected into a separate file for thematic analysis. The key themes and concerns, suggestions and views expressed were then extracted from these files and form part of this report.

3.3.2   The summarised account of each service user group's deliberations was sent to participants for their agreement and they were asked to 'sign off' on the draft as '*a fair and accurate representation of the issues raised and the concerns and suggestions put forward by the group of which I was a member*'. Since participants' names are not to be used, the 'sign off' took the form of a pseudonym or first name of the individual participant's choice. Where any member disagreed with elements of the transcript, this is noted at the end of the summary for the group concerned.

3.3.3   The tapes of the 'Independent' interviews or the detailed notes taken where taping was not done were not transcribed verbatim but were listened to/read up to 3 times by at least one of the researchers. Themes arising under each of the 6 topics covered were noted and participants' verbatim accounts written down when these were particularly illustrative of the issue. Concerns and suggestions for future service development were also noted.

3.3.4   A modified version of the validity and fairness check used for the focus groups was planned for Phase 2. It was to involve contacting a randomly chosen sample of people from the 'Independents' group. However it was quickly evident to all of the interviewers that it would put an unwarranted burden on these participants to ask them to sign-off on a summary which would come to them some time after their interview. Although willing and keen to take part in order to help develop the services, it was clear that many of these participants had to put great personal effort into doing so and we did not wish to impose further on them.

3.3.5   Although just 7 topics are listed in the focus group Discussion Guide and in the interview format used for the Independents, the findings are reported under 9 headings. The added topics were 'Discharge Procedure' and 'Service User Rights and Advocacy'. These issues are reported separately because of the importance they were given by respondents in their accounts of their experiences.

Part 2
Survey Findings

Part II
Survey Findings

Preamble to Part II

The results from Phases I and II of the research project are reported here. Section 4 gives the findings from focus groups 1- 7, the members of which were current or former service users. Section 5 describes the views of the 'Independents', all of whom were current service users. Section 6 looks at data from both phases of the project that indicate the different populations of service users have unique needs, which are not catered for by the mental health services as currently structured.

The eighth focus group was composed of carers of service users and the results of this group are considered in Section 7.

Participants in both Phases gave examples of their experience of 'best practice' by mental health professionals, or arising from the organisation of some aspect of the service. It was also possible to deduce how practice could be changed to better meet users' needs from respondents' accounts of the problems they have encountered when using state mental health services. Thus if service users have difficulty in getting information on the medication prescribed for them when they specifically ask for it, improved practice in this regard would obviously be to give the information in non-technical language and answer any questions the enquirer might have about it. Desirable changes in practice delivery based on respondents' experience are briefly described following the presentation of users' views on each topic under the heading 'Towards Changing Practice'.

The choice of the excerpts used in this chapter and the following chapters in this part of the report was guided by the aim of giving the reader a sense of the kind and range of experiences of the people who use the publicly funded mental health services. Selection from the wealth of information given by all participants was a purely practical necessity. It does not in any way underrate the validity of the views of participants whose words have not been quoted in this chapter.

Section 4
Findings from the Service User Focus Groups

Section 4

Findings from the Service User Focus Groups

4.1.0 Introduction

This chapter uses selected excerpts from the summaries that the members who participated in the focus groups have reviewed and 'signed off' as *'a fair and reasonably accurate account of the deliberations of the group'* in which they took part.

4.1.1 These summaries give a very rich picture of the experience of these current and former service users and the reader is urged to read them in conjunction with this chapter. The summaries are given in Appendix IV.

4.1.2 Square brackets [ ] indicate words added by the principal investigator to clarify the flow of ideas. Curly brackets { } are used to provide context for the speaker's statement.

Topic 1 Initial Contact with the Mental Health Services

Service users' initial contact with the publicly funded mental health service generally occurred in one of two contexts.

○ Persons who initiate contact themselves

○ Persons admitted involuntarily

Persons who initiate contact themselves usually contacted their GP first. Some GPs referred the person to the psychiatric services at this point without attempting to treat the problem.

More generally GPs attempted to give their service users a diagnosis and information on treatment options. A majority of participants noted that GPs were well intentioned and kind.

"...my GP was not dictatorial, he offered suggestions."

" ...I was given two choices with counselling and medication...I wanted to go into hospital and he said 'It is not a good place for you, it is mainly for people who are a danger to themselves, or a danger to you'. He said, 'I wouldn't recommend it'."

"My GP discussed it [medication] with me and explained to me what it was, but I didn't understand why because I felt weepy and all that..."

Where the condition remained severe, the practitioner referred the person to the psychiatric services.

> " …my first contact was with my GP who over a number of weeks …listened to me and spoke to me but eventually referred me to the hospital…"

Service users noted that GPs knowledge of the specifics of a condition was often not detailed and this reduced their effectiveness in treating this patient group.

This lack of specific knowledge seemed to be particularly the case with regard to eating distress and problems with extreme anxiety.

> "He [GP] was very, very nice to me ….but he didn't understand really."

> "I was…diagnosed by my own GP…I think the thing was he was kind of looking at it as a triviality, where I was looking at it as a dire or emergency kind of thing."

> "…I went to my GP and he told me he had no idea of what to do because it wasn't his area…[GP said] I had to go and see a psychiatrist…I didn't want to go near the guy [psychiatrist]…..[because] I had to acknowledge that I had a mental illness and I wasn't going to acknowledge that I had something like that because it was stigmatised."

> "…[GP] said she thought it was an asthma attack that I had.' [and prescribed accordingly]."

> "…After a bit when you kept coming back and…you weren't getting better, with the GP…this is what I found you know 'There is nothing wrong with you [service user's name] and I was getting flustered and anxious….they knew nothing about our situation."

In some cases the consultant psychiatrist seemed not to appreciate the level of distress being experienced by a service user either.

> "..basically I felt that he [psychiatrist] hadn't a clue [how frightening the problem was]. I remember sitting with him and he said to me, 'You know if you just hold your breath you will see that you can actually breathe'. But when you get into a situation where you feel that you can't get your breath…that to me was something [frightening]…you know if they just said…. 'I accept what you're telling me…'"

Three participants went directly to a psychiatrist as private patients when they began to feel unwell. Two respondents said that they were listened to sympathetically.

> "It was a good contact because he [psychiatrist] actually talked to you for half-an-hour."

> "I went to a psychiatrist privately for a while and she was very good ... not much medication and talked about relationships and so on..."

One reported a very negative experience.

> "He left me feeling up-ended. Opened everything up [about problem] and then did nothing about it [at a psychological level]."

Many service users emphasised that it is important that the initial contact with the mental health services should be more hopeful and positive than is often the case.

> "..they never told me that I can get better – I had to discover that for myself...But to have the medical people telling you that [you will not improve/recover] and some of them actually do use the words that 'You have got this for life and you have got to learn to put up with it' - it [saying this] is just not necessary."

> "I was never told by my GP 'You are normal. That is OK – you will get better...There's lots of people like you out there'. I suppose he didn't know about it [that recovery was possible] either you know."

> "You are [vulnerable] and you will be crushed by the slightest thing."

It is important to emphasise that this view was not based on unrealistic expectations.

> " ...I don't believe that any of us can be cured of life 'cos that is what we are talking about, but we have got to learn to deal with our emotions....life goes on and we have to learn how to deal with it."

> "Even though you would have obviously things that wouldn't go always your way, every day is terrific now."

The understanding and optimism of psychiatrists highly skilled in various treatment models had a positive affect on the spirits of service users with whom they worked.

> "Very, very great relief. Fantastic relief...[he said] 'Calm down. I am here for you...' Anyway he reassured me that he would get me better and he did."

Participants noted the importance of early intervention.

> "…I have always said down through the years…[if] I would have been taken out of the situation…maybe none of it [illness] – would have happened."

> "That first meeting with the mental health services took so long…The system has no format for early intervention…if this illness is tackled at the early stages it will not develop into what it does…"

Persons admitted involuntarily were generally brought into contact with the services by a concerned family member acting on their behalf. Some service users were brought to the GP by their family member. Others were brought to a psychiatric facility by a family member, supported by the necessary documentation from the GP. Sometimes the assistance of the Gardai had to be obtained if the service user was in a particularly distressed state.

Persons admitted involuntarily did not always recollect the details of their admission, but they recalled the experience in general as being traumatic and to involve inordinate force.

> "…I thought I was going to a nursing home and then I realised where I was going and it was very terrifying…I wouldn't go in like and they had to force me in…"

> "I didn't cooperate at all because I was kept in against my will. I don't like my freedom being taken away from me and I'd fight. I'd fight anyone who would take my freedom off me."

> "… The place kind of freaked me out {and service user left without being discharged} but I was forcefully taken back and I remember these two big psychiatric nurses taking off my clothes and I had this impulse to just jump out the window. I'm not quite sure why they had to be so brutal but they certainly were…"

> "I have seen people come into the hospital especially in [named secure location]. Bundled in and the person would be talking or shouting…giving out and all of this. Nobody spoke. Nobody says, 'Take it easy, take it easy, calm down. Have a cup of tea'. No – that's never done. Only hauled in the room, stripped down and injected…People who are in trouble! I mean if they weren't in some kind of trouble they wouldn't be there in the first place."

The lack of any attempt to prepare a person for admission and to give information on their situation was noted, although participants did acknowledge that they were not always in a psychological state to fully grasp and use this information.

> "I knew I was unwell…the GP…said would I go to [local psychiatric facility]. Now I didn't think I was going to be staying there…They [medical personnel] wanted to keep me and I didn't want to stay at all. I didn't cooperate at all but like I signed the form because I was persuaded to sign the voluntary form."

"...I went to the psychiatric hospital and my abiding memory is sitting endlessly, I was left here for an hour, two hours and I was pacing up and down this little room...You know why weren't they interviewing me? I didn't really know what was happening..."

"Nobody explained why I was there [in the inpatient facility]."

"When a person is admitted first maybe they may not want their treatment explained. But as they begin to recover – yes, they do want to know..."

Participants were also concerned that their families were not given enough support at the time of a service user's admission.

"They left my [spouse] in hallway of that hospital...and nobody came near her. And she's crying...and she had to get on the train back to [home location] that night...and nobody put their arms around her, nobody addressed her, nobody came near her..."

Towards Changing Practice in Initial Contact and Admission

Access to mental health professionals needs to be made easier and less stigmatising. GPs are the obvious link into the health care system for most people and a referral from a GP is necessary to access the publicly funded system. However GPs do not and cannot be expected to have the degree of specialised pharmacological and psychological knowledge that developments in mental health care have brought in recent years. Nor have they the time to deliver these services as part of their general medical practice. Consequently mental health professionals with these skills must be part of the primary health care system to facilitate early and non-stigmatising intervention.

Involuntary admission must be made less traumatic and more dignified for the service user, and less troubling and difficult for their families and for the professionals involved. Service users were quite realistic about the need for such admissions on occasion but were concerned at the sometimes harrowing nature of the experience.

Voluntary admissions too need to be dealt with promptly and sensitively, taking account of the anxious concern of the service user and his/her accompanying family.

The impact of an encouraging attitude on the part of the professional should not be underestimated. In this respect, mental health professionals with specialist therapeutic skills can offer welcome reassurance to a service user. Participants felt that in their wish to be realistic, professionals were inclined to emphasise only the enduring nature of some ailments, thus creating pessimism among service users.

Topic 2 Treatment and Therapy

Medication is the main form of treatment at primary care and within the mental health service itself.

> "[Treatment is] definitely drugs based. Totally."

> "…You get a prescription at the end of it…"

This emphasis on medication as the treatment of first choice meant that consultations with the psychiatric specialist or NCHDs focused on clinical symptoms rather than on the lived experiences of the service user.

> "Are you sleeping? Are you eating? And 'How are you feeling?…Generally they were the questions. There was no room for discussing things…everybody goes into a psychiatric hospital with a story. It is emotional, mental pain of some sort, but the story ends on the first day. Medication begins and pharmaceutical companies take over."

> "….I would like them [medical personnel] to listen to my problem – what I am worried about. What has upset me. Rather than not only the fact that I am not sleeping or that I am agitated or something. That is all they concern themselves with - the symptoms but not the cause. And one would expect that after a time in the hospital the cause would be discussed before sending one back out to where the problem originated. But that is what happens – they [service users] are sent back out to where the problem originated and the problem is not fully discussed."

> "I keep hearing the words, 'Keep taking the medication'. Most people would hear that…[but] some people need reassurance. They need to be understood because you can be very isolated… and you are dying to tell someone about your problems, like you know."

Many participants were not negative about medication, although all but two participants had concerns about it being the predominant or sole treatment option.

> "…I get periods of about eight months when…I would be fairly [well] but I would say like if it weren't (sic) for the medication…I'd be in hospital a lot longer."

> "Very good, I find it good. More [helpful] than anything else. I had a lot of information first before I went on it…I had read a lot about the possible side effects. So I was kind of ready for it. I was surprised at how it has helped."

> "…they [clinicians] have given me a very good medication…I am very, very thankful to them…they discussed it with me and I am very happy with it now."

"I do believe that there is a place when people are in crisis for medication...because dreadful suffering goes on when you are either very high or very low, hearing voices or whatever. There is awful suffering and I don't believe in suffering if you can stop it. But [if medication is over-used] I think it is dangerous."

"So medication, I have a very high regard for it and I accept it has a place in recovery. Its is just that it is not good enough anymore to hand it out to people without there being a...proper type of consultation with the other option there... [other treatment options should also be considered]."

These service users also emphasised that medication often came at a price in terms of their quality of life.

" ...they [tablets] absolutely numb, they numb, they turn you into a robot really."

"I was on medication for almost 20 years and it just kept me in a zombie state for that time....I was zonked out....Like imagine if it happened to you – imagine if all your gifts were taken away from you and all the ways you – the things you enjoyed most in life were all taken away from you!"

"I put on tons [of weight] but what can you do? It is a side effect of being on the medication. Its like being miserable and depressed or being fat and happy. The lesser of the two evils, isn't it! It definitely is"!

"The medication affects your ability to work."

"My memory isn't great from all the medication."

"I suppose Lithium sometimes kept me from going high but it kept me at a low keel. I wasn't reaching my intelligence, creativity, and things like that....life's gotten lame."

"...You felt nothing then [on medication]. You wouldn't feel like laughing. You wouldn't feel like crying. You just didn't feel. You wouldn't feel excited. You wouldn't feel."

As well as being concerned that medication was so often the only treatment option offered, group members considered that it was sometimes over-prescribed:-

" If you start getting depressed over that [contemplating the future] they give you more medication, I mean it is a vicious circle like."

" ....every time I went they put me on a new [medication]...they just said, 'Right, you are on this as well now'..."

That its mode of action was not fully understood by the medical personnel prescribing it:

"I would wake up on a regular basis…with these sort of hallucinatory thoughts…I thought this was the mental illness and I was going to a psychiatrist telling him this every time. Then I read up after when I got back to myself [felt better] that this [hallucinatory experience] is a side effect of taking the drugs. And he never copped it…like how would somebody who is supposed to be an expert in the field not know that, you know?"

"It [expected improvement following medication] never happened…I said it [to clinician] but they just say – it is kind of ironic really – they kind of say, 'You should be doing more things keeping yourself active'… That is ironic – they put you on medication and then if it doesn't work they say, 'Oh it is because you are not busy enough….."

That side-effects were not always discussed or taken seriously by the consultants/NCHDs:

"Several times I have mentioned a certain side effect and she said, 'Oh I have never heard of that before' but has still not made a note of it…And I know there is a space in the back of the book to notify the pharmaceutical companies."

"…I would ask the doctors about the side effects and you could see them getting annoyed. It was a case of these are the side effects and we have to state them by law, we have to write them down but you don't really have to worry about them. And I saw one of the side effects was death, and I would worry about that! So I said that to the doctor and he thought I was being smart and I said, 'I am not [being smart]. I am genuinely worried about taking these tablets' and you could see he was getting annoyed and irritated…I went to another doctor and I went to another chemist and again they were all kind of flippant – 'We have to state them [side effects] by law'"

"You found out [about the side effects of the medication] by something having happened to yourself…you would have a patch or blob [on skin] or shake or tremor or whatever, and only then – when you complain to the nurse – the doctor would say, 'Oh that's the side effects'. And they dismiss the side effects."

And that many medical personnel had little or no interest in working with service users to reduce or otherwise modify the dose taken:

"For the last two years I haven't been on it [medication] at all. But I have had to do that all by myself….."

"I have one problem that I would like to see my medication changed because of the side effects of my medication. And I have said it to the doctors and this is going back about eight months ago now. And they never changed the medication, [they] said wait…I keep waiting [but] it hasn't happened."

"…if you are an alcoholic there are places you can go, like you know. Some successful place…detoxing…There are places…[for] people who go on drugs voluntarily, other drugs. There is nothing for people who are on psychiatric drugs and who want to get off them. And then they make the mistake of coming off them too fast and then it is seen as their illness [rather] than the side effects of coming off medication."

A number of service users emphasised that their criticism was not levelled at individual medical personnel, but at the system that had trained them and the system within which they worked.

"I am not blaming the GPs or the psychiatrists…I believe that it is the system. It is the way they are trained and its the system that they have to go along with that I feel is greatly at fault. It is nothing personal at all."

"My GP is…he is a good family doctor, this is not a judgement of him…he just didn't know [about anxiety states]."

{Speaking about the need for professionals to keep up to date after qualification a speaker said} "I don't have an expectation that a doctor is going to cure me, but I do have an expectation that they will educate themselves and know what is there for a common complaint…"

Those consultant psychiatrist and GPs who worked in partnership with service users to reduce or optimise medication were especially appreciated by participants.

"I think there is a bit of a change in the attitude…a couple of years ago the last time I went to a clinic, I was contemplating changing my medication because of the side effects and he [consultant] actually gave me a choice. 'Its up to you' he said."

"The GP I have is good. In terms of a treatment plan, a lot of it has been 'We will see if its working or not working' but at least she is nice about it…I feel she is very committed you know. It has taken about three years to get the cocktail [combination of drugs] right for me…and I don't consider that it is totally right, but I think she has been very patient and watched it very closely. It certainly helps [when the clinician is engaged with the service user]."

"I do take medication…but I must say that I was very pleased with my own GP because he actually brought me down…[reduced dose significantly]."

The absence of or difficulty in accessing other therapies for those who would find them of benefit is seen as a major deficit in the service.

'It would be wonderful to talk to someone one-to-one with [a] psychotherapy type of therapeutic background rather than a doctor. Obviously let the psychiatrists talk about their medication. That's fine. I see that as a necessity as well but what I don't see [is] that there can be a contradiction between taking medicine and [other therapies]…"

Participants noted that if they wished to avail of psychological therapies they had to do so privately and this put them under considerable financial strain.

> "…if I want to get a bit of psychotherapy like I go to a psychotherapist privately…because I don't think I get that from the health service…"

> "I wish they would bring therapists into the actual services and allow people the option without having to pay. It is tough enough going through what you are going through without being financially broke as well…"

> "…for a counsellor or something 50 euro-an-hour is beyond people who are on disability."

They also noted that the publicly funded mental health service did not offer choice of therapists (whether medically qualified or with psychology or other therapeutic qualifications).

> "…but if you go in as a [public] patient you are given this person [therapist] and [if] it [the relationship] doesn't work…you are vulnerable."

> "And if you are not getting on with somebody you should at least have the right to go to someone with whom you can get on."

> {Speaker is addressing another participant who had been criticised for asking to change clinician} "And say it to them [ask for the change] without them telling you that you're being whatever [critical remark] he said to you."

Participants pointed out that no one approach or therapist will suit everybody.

> " …she [counsellor/psychologist] wasn't for me at all…I went through a lot of different things before I found the right one."

> "I went to a behavioural psychologist and she told me that I was fine. I didn't think I was a bit fine!"

> "I went to TM for a while…it absolutely did nothing for me, you know…. [Service user then tried hypnotherapy]…I had three sessions…he [therapist] said …. I wasn't a candidate for hypnosis."

> {After an negative experience with counselling a service user noted} "I subsequently went to another counsellor. It was the best thing I did…So that was a good experience."

Service users also noted that there might be a 'readiness' factor when people can most benefit from psychological therapy and/or that they may need to access it more than once or on an 'as needed' basis over time.

> "…[group therapy]…in the day hospital [was not helpful]. And the doctor told my Mum that I was therapy resistant! But later in [named other location] I was different [and got more benefit]. It [the therapy] was a lot more structured."

> "…and everybody is at different stages…so I don't know if it is taken on board that people are at different stages and sometimes I might have to do something three times to get what I needed out of it…"

Mental health service planners and mental health professionals in the publicly funded service appear to be quite unclear about the value of the contribution made by non-medical interventions to service users' care. Such interventions are not an integral part of the publicly funded mental health care service. This is evidenced by the generally limited range and sporadic availability of these services.

> "They have bits of it [occupational therapy] and it goes grand for a time and you look forward to the next time. Like Yoga was on and I was looking forward to the next week and [the next week] the girl that was doing it was gone."

> "You'd have something and [it was] great and then it was gone. Its even more frustrating because you have a bit of it and [it is gone]."

> "[In the private mental health service] there is an art room and a pottery room and there is a crafts [room], and there is a stress management [programme] and there is a mood disorder [programme]…[In the public service] it was just one big room and it was all cluttered together and you couldn't focus…"

> "…there is a stark contrast between say [location X] and [location Y] {within the same Board mental health service}. [Location Y] is really top class in comparison…occupational therapy classes…the 'stay well' classes and how to cope with living on the outside, those classes…they had a sports room…So I am glad I am living in the [Location Y catchment area]."

> "…And they do baking or cooking. That's good, that's very good. But there is not enough of it."

Services such as occupational therapy are sometimes delivered by people not trained in the speciality, and the activities included under this heading are questionable.

> "…so this Thursday we're going to have a quiz. 'Jack and Jill went up the hill to fetch – what'? …But its…outrageous – the insult to your intelligence as to what these people ask you to do in the name of 'Occupational Therapy'"

> "…it lasted for about half-an-hour and they read the horoscopes. You know…when you think about it as a way of getting people out of themselves, its not that great you know."

> "Newspaper reading for half-an-hour. They have Bingo and things like that. They have relaxation tapes and they do a bit of cookery some days…and they have a bit of timber work. But do you see there's only room for a certain number of people [at these activities]."

Such activities as are available are poorly matched to the changing needs of service users as they recover.

> "You were so zonked [from medication] you couldn't concentrate on anything. I was doing the simplest things that a child would do and they were hard for me to do… [but with recovery] Bingo and snakes and ladders. They are an insult to your intelligence!"

> "Occupational therapy, sheltered workshops. As far as I am concerned they serve their purpose but they take a long time to do…and the work can be very boring. I think there should be a limit in terms of the time you spend in them and the aim should be to move the person on. It is a dead end. It is a dead end!"

Towards Changing Practice in Treatment and Therapy

The range of interventions needs to be widened beyond the medical treatment option.

The role of psychological and social factors (e.g., pattern of thinking and acting; interpersonal and intra-familial relationships) in service users' lives and the impact these factors have on their mental well being must be directly addressed as an integral part of the therapeutic intervention offered to service users.

Service planners need to recognise the above point and ensure that appropriately qualified mental health professionals are available throughout the different catchment areas, and that these professionals are adequately resourced to deliver a sustained (rather than sporadic) quality service.

Partnership between the clinician and the service user is a key element in changing practice. Although some service users felt that avoiding discussion of drug side effects and of their illness generally might be meant to protect them, the approach was seen as 'paternalistic' and was considered unsatisfactory by all respondents.

As part of their on-going treatment plan for their individual service users, clinicians should seriously consider the reduction or changing a service user's medication (even if only in the short term) in order to minimise side effects as much as possible. Psychiatric professionals as a group might consider debating having the goal of coming off medication completely (which some participants had achieved on their own) as a therapeutic aim in the treatment of mental illness generally.

Persons using the state funded mental health services must have the opportunity to change their therapist if necessary. This is crucial to a quality mental health service since inter-personal relationships are as fundamental a part of the nature of mental illness as is any physical or chemical factor. It is unrealistic to think that therapists and service users will 'hit it off' and be interpersonally compatible in all instances.

Topic 3 Experience of the Inpatient Service

Relationship with Mental Health Professionals.

As might be deduced from the finding on treatment and therapy, engagement between service users and clinicians tended to be remote.

> "…even direct questioning like; they wouldn't reply. They kind of evade the answer or change the subject."

> "They don't know you in the first place. He [consultant] never knew me. He never asked me any questions to find out who I was. So how could he diagnose me?"

Longer term users of the state funded mental health service noted that there has been an improvement in the relationship between nursing staff and clients over the years.

> "They [nurses] talk more about the psychology of what you are going through now than they did 10 years ago…when I went into the hospital first a long time ago if you didn't get up in the morning the clothes were pulled off you and the nurses wouldn't be beyond giving you a thump…Whereas nowadays they treat it as though it were an illness like any other illness and you are entitled to sympathy and compassion…"

Some current members of the nursing profession were highly praised:

> "…nurse who would listen for a very, very long time and listen a few times, and that's what one needs."

> "They [staff nurses] took time to talk to you and play cards…"

{A service user who was fearful of admission was encouraged by the nursing staff as follows} " Come in and look around if you want to. Come in and see what the ward is like…It is not closed. You don't go 'round in 'straight jackets' and you can wear your own clothes….So initially the warmth from the nursing staff [helped]."

"…they pride themselves that if you want to talk to somebody they will talk to you and give you a pep talk…"

Others were felt to be disinterested and dismissive:

"They don't seem to have any kind of feeling for people at all like. I mean really and truly a bit of kindness goes a long way and that's all people need."

"You meet some lovely nurses but you are also going to meet people who are putting their day in…that is all they are doing."

"I was admitted at lunch time [and didn't feel like eating] The ward sister said, 'You're going to have to learn to eat sometime you know! {Speaker was experiencing eating disorder}.

Participants were philosophical about this mixture of positive and negative approaches by nursing staff.

"…there are some people not suited to certain jobs…there are some dedicated nurses there like, that – who are just made for it. You get some guards aren't meant to be guards. Some nurses aren't supposed to nurses like; in all different professions [you get a mixture]."

Group members felt that the organisational structure and ambiance of the mental health care system worked against nurses having a more therapeutic contact with them.

"One nurse might have four or five patients with whom she is supposed to chat during the day. But right – you might have a chat with that nurse or you might ask her if you could have a chat and she would tell you, 'I'm busy now' or 'In five minutes'…you might get to talk to her and you mightn't get to talk to her at all…they are so busy running here and running there and there's nothing to do but give out drugs and book work…"

"There's no or very little interaction between the nurse and the patients…They do the beds or whatever they have to do but they don't tend to interact with the patients."

"…They've [psychiatric nurses] got so used to the idea that you can do nothing for these patients that they've developed…they don't take much interest in you."

Respondents noted that the potential for night nursing staff to interact in a therapeutic way with service users was ignored.

> "…I couldn't sleep and I got up and I was just walking down the corridor…but you are told to go back to bed immediately…I said to myself …I could do with someone to talk to… Even if it is the middle of the night especially - you are in hospital; you are there for a reason and it is to do with suffering and your suffering does not go away from ten o'clock at night until eight o'clock in the morning…"

> "…I knew somebody that was on the ward and she got up three nights in a row, and of course in the middle of the night is when you feel worst. And the nurses – there were two nurses at the nurses' station having a conversation and [they] told her to go back to bed and she was really distressed…"

The relative absence of other professions from the service meant that few comments were made on the nature of their interaction with users of the inpatient service. Thus no reliable patterns emerged. The impact of care and catering staff on the quality of the inpatient experience in general was similarly rarely commented on. The impact of other patients is dealt with in Section 6 where the difference in needs between different clinical conditions is dealt with in some detail.

Special Problems with the Inpatient Therapeutic Regime

Participants identified enforced compliance with the medical treatment regime, and the use of seclusion and restraint when a service user was extremely distressed as areas requiring urgent and creative attention. Respondents who had experience of both public and private services noted that these problems are common to both.

> "When I refuse a drug from the nurse she would say, 'Oh you have to take it…You are written up for it". And if I still don't take it I am assaulted by anything up to five male and female nurses, put on a bed…and injected with a most painful inter-muscular injection which renders me in the depths of depression."

> "…in society like, most things you know are questioned now about that…like even in the classroom like, the children [ask questions]. But we are people…to be treated like this [rights ignored and compliance required]. "We have no rights at all, ya. Imagine it!"

> "…there must be another way of doing this. Not a completely open door so that distressed patients can wander around the roads but not a lock up way that takes away the dignity [of a person]."

> "We are not criminals, prisoners have more power."

Daily Life in the Inpatient Facility

A majority of participants described day-to-day life in the inpatient facility as dreary, de-skilling, and anti-therapeutic and likely to promote institutionalisation when admissions were lengthy or frequent.

"You're sitting around on your own usually…most people would be depressed so they're not very talkative to each other. They sit in watching – the television is on all day."

"No garden. No place to go outside. There is a place that they call it a conservatory but there are no plants, and it is inside as well. You know, it is not outside [so there is no] fresh air" .

"If you don't smoke and don't like TV there is nothing else to do. That is basically all that happens all day long – smoking and watching TV. And you are basically just walking up and down the corridor…it is just soul-destroying really."

"There are no vacuums in life. You are never doing nothing. The mind is always working. So when there is nothing to do and you are cut off from the outside world, you are working on yourself and you are [doing] all this self analysis. And in my case all that work was negatives – that I can't do this and I can't do that. And that left me powerless."

"…I couldn't do my shopping, I can't go to the chemist…I can't [do my cooking] and when I came out I was unable to do these simple things…"

"I was in a locked ward one time and I said, 'This is great…I have a bed, have sheets, I don't have to worry about the world, I can stay here forever'…I got used to it then like. Which is dangerous, 'cos that wouldn't have been my true character. I was a free person [before hospitalisation]."

The lack of continuity of care was noted as a particular problem by all participants.

"…the same doctor that you might build up…some kind of relationship with…they changed so often. I had this new doctor …and all he did was prescribe. He didn't listen to me…just prescribed the same drugs that I was on before which were really causing me terrible trouble…"

The Physical and Psychological Environment

Participants with long-term experience of the publicly funded service noted that the physical environment had improved, although ongoing maintenance was sometimes lacking.

> "...the conditions there were just positively Victorian and it was just filthy. [Over time] there is no comparison..."

> "The physical surroundings might be getting cleaner...everything is clinically clean..."

> "...but the surroundings now...they were drab, dreary..."

The relative absence of privacy when meeting visitors and during intimate self-care was difficult for most participants.

> " I wanted privacy to talk to my own father and I didn't have it. It was in the ward he was talking to me, like."

> "...[The visitors' room is] a small locked room...and sometimes there are three sets of visitors there...with no privacy and there's a camera looking down on you..."

> "What really got to me as an inpatient was the total lack of privacy, not even being able to go to the loo on your own...Having two nurses there when you were having a bath..."

> "...it takes a lot of getting used to...in that the toilets aren't closed from a girl's point of view and they are right next to the nurses' station and the doors don't close...they don't lock so you have patients walking in..."

The absence of physical exercise and access to fresh air by spending time outside the ward was specifically emphasised by many participants.

> "...you are not physically unwell and you are able [to exercise]. Any kind of physical outlet is very beneficial to you."

> "...I got no exercise for nearly 8 months. So its bad."

> "...exercise is very important all right. The garden – I found that very therapeutic."

Being required to wear night attire rather than day clothes was experienced as de-personalising.

> "You have to wear your pyjamas because...I suppose they think if you are in your pyjamas you are less inclined to escape."

> "You will stay in your nightdress until they decide you are ready to give you your

> own clothes and nobody wants [to be] walking around in a mixed ward in their nightdress. It is a bit de-humanising."

The lack of spiritual support in one secure setting was commented on.

> " …They probably [thought] we were unwell or we didn't have a belief maybe or something. But it was never asked….some questions should be asked in relation to God or spiritual belief or whatever. I think it is relevant."

Towards Changing Practice in the Inpatient Service

Improving practice in inpatient care would include:

More personal engagement by clinicians with the service users in their care.

The realisation of the therapeutic potential of the nurse-patient relationship – particularly in the case of night nursing staff – which is currently being under-exploited because of traditional work practices and an emphasis on administration.

The development and implementation of a programme of therapeutic and recreational activities graded to meet the level of need of service users at different stages of recovery, to counteract the anti-therapeutic vacuum that occurs when service users have nothing constructive to do.

Examination of the research literature and consultation with service users and mental health service providers and professionals (in Ireland and elsewhere) to determine more satisfactory ways of dealing with acceptance of treatment and extreme service user distress, and with security while minimising the intrusion on users' privacy and personal dignity.

Ensuring a clean, well-maintained, and pleasantly cheerful physical environment so that service users can feel at ease, comfortable and encouraged by their surroundings.

The opportunity for physical exercise and access to the outside to promote and maintain service users' good physical health as well as their psychological wellbeing.

Consideration of the spiritual needs of individual service users.

Topic 4 Discharge Procedure

Most of the participants did not comment in any detail on the discharge procedure which seemed to be a mainly administrative process. As such it went more or less smoothly as the following excerpts show.

"I have found it good in all my discharges...I've been given enough medication for one week and an outpatient appointment to follow..."

"They made sure I had a lift...They were concerned that I didn't drive myself because of the medication."

"They gave me two days medication and then they forgot...to give me a prescription so I ended up with an old prescription and there was changes that weren't in the old prescription..."

"...you know you hand in your personal belongings when you come in and I forgot [to ask for] my keys...so he [taxi driver] drove me all the way back...and I ended up paying 17 quid – 17 euros, because I forgot my keys...they could have got all my belongings together. It wasn't entirely up to me to think of every item that I gave them."

Some facilities gave prior notice of discharge to the service user and arranged for a weekend to be spent at home before leaving the facility permanently. However the following extracts show that service users probably need to be equipped with specific coping skills and to have some assurance of professional support in the community as well.

"Towards the end of my stay in hospital I was told my psychiatrist had said I should spend a weekend at home. This was a very frightening step for me to take and I wanted to talk to my psychiatrist about it. I was told she was gone on holidays...I went on to have a panic attack as a result of that incident."

" I said, 'Look if I feel panicky...will there be a chance to get in [readmitted]? And he [discharging professional] said, 'You rely too much on the hospital service'."

"...I met him [Community Psychiatric Nurse] before I left...[my discharge planning was] very human and very thorough."

"And in my last admission...I was told if I need to go back in between that week, just come up and visit...if you feel it is too much to be out...just those words of support were enough. I didn't need to go back but I found that very nice."

Towards Changing Practice at Discharge

The discharge process could be improved in the following ways.

Notification to the service user of date of discharge with discussion of his/her concerns about returning to home, work and the community generally.

Where necessary suggesting and helping the service user to develop strategies to cope with anticipated problems.

CPN meeting with the service user prior to the latter's returning home and if possible CPN involvement in pre-discharge preparation.

Assuring the service user that support can be accessed at unit, Day Centre or Social Work/CPN service should the need arise.

A note to the Reader on Topics 5/6 Experience of Day Hospital/Day Centre Services

Day hospitals are intended to offer the range of services available in inpatient facilities but persons who attend the day hospital go home each evening. Day centres aim to offer a range of services such as drop in support facilities which may offer social support, single session counselling, clinical advice, advice on rehabilitation, and various organised activities such as relaxation sessions, stress or anxiety management programmes etc. Focus group participants were not always sure whether the service they used was best described as a day hospital or a day centre.

As Principal Investigator I have exercised my judgement in deciding to allocate participants' comments to one or the other type of facility. This action is important because it appears that the focus group service users find day centres to be more satisfactory than day hospitals. The reader is asked to bear this action in mind when assessing the findings on the next two topics.

Topic 5 Experience of the Day Hospital

Approximately18% of the participants had day hospital experience. Most service users received follow-up care through an outpatient clinic and through the Community Psychiatric Nursing service, (discussed later).

The availability of a day hospital service varied across catchment areas and the quality of the activities on offer were also variable.

> "It is very, very good. It is just a great support."

> "…they [staff] were very well meaning. It was not that they didn't care. They were very well meaning but I found it…sort of vague. The whole thing was very vague. I would prefer something more structured and focused."

> "Again it was unstructured, it wasn't well organised. You just had the dinner in the middle of the day. That's the only certainty you had each day."

> "… I found that [day hospital] very good. It was like a stepping stone between hospital and real life you know. But then once…[that ended there was very little]."

Towards Changing Practice in the Day Hospital

Day hospital services are most satisfactory and productive when they offer (a) well structured programmes, and when (b) those programme offer a variety of therapeutic activities suited to the changing needs of service users as they progress to recovery.

Topic 6 Experience of the Day Centre and Ancillary Services

Again only a minority of the focus group participants had experience of the day centre services and of ancillary support services such at the National Training and Development Institute (NTDI).

Service users with day centre experience found it satisfactory, although they noted that places there are in short supply.

> " …I have a good experience of the day hospital (sic)…a nurse there and the occupational therapist kind of got together…they kind of took me for a couple of sessions and it just did so much good. It was a great relief…they were so caring."

"…and the staff there…they were all caring. There was no such thing as I am staff and you are the patient. [It was] Lively and nice. You could enjoy it….You could have a chat and make a cup of tea and cook your lunch…[Although] it was quite boring at times, especially in the afternoons."

" …you have to be referred there and some people might get going – might get there every Monday. Other people might get there every Tuesday, so there isn't enough. If you are only going to a day centre on a Monday, what do you do for the rest of the week?"

Occupational guidance and assistance for service users to return to work was sometimes available. Although some services were considered to be excellent there is a need to improve their standard in some locations.

"Rehabilitation – especially a fabulous social worker…and through them I got a life and a career…"

"[NTDI course] Fresh Start…I said …there is no way I could do a course like that because it is 9 – 4.30pm and he [education officer] said, 'Would you try it for two days…? and then I did the six months…There is fierce understanding in there in that particular place. It is a very safe environment…"

"There is a company…And what you have is you have a job coach and they go to the employer with you…They probably tell them [employer] [about your disability] before you have the interview. So that is a support is there…They are very friendly and they would do anything for you. They are a definite asset for anyone who has a disability of any kind, ya."

"I made it clear that I was going out of my mind with boredom which was aggravating the depression and the rest of it. I said, 'I need to get back into the workforce. I don't care how I get back into it, I said'…and I haven't heard from her [placement officer] since."

Towards Changing Practice in the Day Centre

Further development of activities and programme.

Assurance of a uniformly high standard of occupational guidance across all catchment areas to assist service users to plan their return to appropriate full or part-time employment.

Day centre services need to be sufficient to meet the demand for them so that all service users who need them can have access and can have this for as many days as needed during each week.

Topic 7 **The Outpatient Experience**

Attendance at the outpatient clinic is the primary form of ongoing care offered to service users. This service as it exists is judged to be unsatisfactory by the majority of participants. There are three interrelated reasons for this.

O Lack of continuity of care

O Insufficient time for the consultation

O Multiple appointments for the same time

The following verbatim quotes give the predominant flavour of service users' views.

On lack of continuity of care

> " …when you come out it is very [difficult to see the consultant]. The registrar is changed every six months."

> " …It is difficult when you meet all these different people [and] you have to…tell it all out again…it gets very, very tiresome to have to explain the same thing…You feel like carrying a tape recorder around with you and just say, 'Play that there!'"

> "And it is very seldom that you would see your consultant at outpatients' clinics. It is usually a junior doctor and a different doctor each time. No continuity at all."

> "In terms of outpatients …you've no guarantee of meeting the same psychiatrist or the same SHO even."

On insufficient time for the consultation

> "Two or three minutes…and you are waiting two or three hours for that two or three minutes."

> {The speaker describes the format and tone of a typical interchange in the OP clinic}. "…I don't see any benefit in 'How are you, do you want your medication? OK, and how are things? 'Do you know anything about me? Have you read my file? 'No'. So you are not going to [cover] seven years of work in 15 minutes…I wouldn't have a high regard for the person. I would just say like 'Can I have my prescription? I wouldn't have a high respect for them."

> "You would end up not saying three words to them." [About service user's current situation]

On multiple appointments

> "I think it is very wrong the way when you go up as an outpatient they call your name out. Your full name and your surname to everybody who is there in the waiting room…If they could have one [a system] where there could be a number…so there is no need to call out your name and address in front of everybody."

> "There's no time. I mean people who haven't been in the system don't realise how little time is actually given to people. I mean you have about 40 patients between about half-nine and twelve o'clock."

Other community-based support was thin on the ground and the professionals involved were often over-stretched.

> "…But as for the number of [community psychiatric] nurses [and] social workers [it] is very limited and there's such a wide [catchment] area that they are usually fire-fighting. You only see them in a crisis, like."

> "There was a social worker but…she is really busy. But she is a very nice person and she is as helpful as she can be…"

> "I would think community nurses are very, very important…they need specialist training for people coming out of a psychiatric ward…"

> "Social workers only come in when things are gone really bad. They don't come in earlier. They come in when it is too late and then we're really in trouble."

Social support and welfare systems need to have procedures that are more flexible and speedy in their response to the varying social, work or benefit related needs of these service users.

> "[because] I'm on medication I wouldn't work as fast as other people…if I go to my accountant and tell him that's what I earned for the year he looks at me and says… 'You couldn't survive on that…If I send that into the Revenue they're going to be asking questions as well'… And they have…And you still go through it every time. …I could pack in work and go on disability which I don't want to do…I want to stay working. [The system] doesn't want to deal with it [when someone wants to work as much as they are able]…"

Towards Changing Practice in Outpatient Care and Community Support

The structure and operation of outpatient clinics should be addressed so that:

Continuity of care is assured and time need no longer be spent skimming notes or taking details that are already on file.

There is sufficient consultation time to allow service users to talk about their concerns and receive advice as well as a prescription from their doctor.

Discretion and confidentiality are observed by using a system other than calling out service users names in a crowded waiting room.

Service user waiting time before seeing their consultant is decreased by not scheduling many appointments for the same time or too close together.

CPN and social worker support should be significantly developed so that service users' difficulties can be dealt with before they reach crisis levels.

Social support and welfare systems should be streamlined so that they are easier for service users to understand and less cumbersome for them to use.

Topic 8 Treatment Plan

The absence of treatments and therapies other than medication make this a somewhat moot issue in its most positive sense.

> "…they give you drugs and that is it."

> "I understand what you are saying [asking about a treatment plan] but no; any part of my treatment [other than medication] would have been my own initiative."

Towards Changing Practice in Treatment Planning

Changes in practice in relation to the use of medication with service users whose problems may be persistent were noted in **Topic 2** and this form of practice should become the norm.

The absence of the ready availability of non-pharmacological therapies must be addressed so that treatment planning may become a reality in its fullest sense.

Topic 9 Service User Rights and Advocacy

The rights of service users to information about their condition, to be consulted about their treatment and to give or withhold their consent in relation to it and various other matters are all ill defined as far as participants were concerned. The following extracts illustrate the issues as they see them.

> "If you are committed [involuntary admission] [your] rights as a citizen are waived."

> "They [medical personnel] don't hand the power over to you, like. They take it all away from you."

> "I was sectioned at the time [patient's admission was involuntary]so again – about rights – I wasn't given my rights either [never had rights explained]. That is very upsetting."

Service users with experience in advocacy noted that the publicly funded mental health service is unwelcoming and possibly somewhat hostile to this activity.

> " ...a person might request that I'd go to their doctor with them...[but] it is basically up to the doctor if they allow me to accompany the person or not."

> "...when I went in to see her [consultant] she had all her students in a room like this...and I was there like to confront her with all this entourage around her...she was making [service user who sought advocacy] out to be a bully ...And she was trying to say as well that she could see our point of view but we couldn't see her point of view..."

Towards Changing Practice in Service User Rights and Advocacy

A partnership approach involving service users as well as relevant others is one of the guiding values of the Mental Health Commission.

As mentioned above in the discussion of acceptance of treatment, security matters and the use of seclusion and restraint under **Topic 3**, examination of the research literature and consultation with all concerned parties should be part of the Commission's deliberations.

It would naturally be advisable that the approach and ethos to user rights and advocacy should be one of conciliation and negotiation rather than of confrontation and litigation.

Whatever policy and procedures emerge from the work of the Mental Health Commission, it would be essential to ensure that service user advocates and the mental health professionals and programme managers who will be involved in implementing them be given sufficient appropriate training.

Section 5
Findings from the 'Independent' Interviews

Section 5

Findings from the 'Independent' Interviews

5.1.0   Introduction

5.1.1   The views of the 48 current users of the publicly funded mental health services are presented in this section. Respondents were not members of any mutual help or advocacy group at the time of interview. The approximate median duration of their period of contact with the mental health services was five years with a range of under one month to 20 years[13]. Table 5.1 gives the key descriptive statistics for the 'Independents'.

Table 5.1 Characteristics of the 'Independents'					
Gender		**Age**		**Duration of Contact with Service**	
Male	Female	18-30yrs.	30+yrs.	<3yrs.	>3yrs.
24	24	14	34	28	20

5.1.2   Interviewees gave their views under each of the topics covered with the focus groups. Forty-two participants allowed their contribution to be tape recorded. Six participants preferred to have their views recorded by the interviewer in notes made during the interview.

5.1.3   Square brackets [ ] indicate words added by the principal investigator to clarify the flow of ideas. Curly brackets { } are used to provide context for the speaker's statement.

---

13   *We did not have or seek access to service users' records and participants generally could give only an approximate time for their length of contact with the services when this was longer than 4 years.*

Topic 1 Initial Contact with the Mental Health Services

Table 5.2 gives the pattern of Initial Contact for the 'Independent' participants.

Table 5.2 Pattern of 'Independent' Initial Contact with Mental Health Services		
Contact Point	Initiated by	
	Self	Family Member
GP	24	15
Psychiatrist	4	2

Point of contact was not clear in 3 cases.

The GP was the first point of contact for most participants. Where initial contact was with a psychiatrist or psychologist/counsellor this was privately funded by the service user or his/her family. The point of contact and/or who initiated it was not clear in the cases.

Experience with GPs was mixed.

"My GP was very understanding. He put me in contact with the hospital…"

"She…was very helpful…and when I returned [from hospital] she told me to keep in touch with her, to keep coming back to her."

"My GP is brilliant, really brilliant. He'd listen to me for an hour."

"I found my [new] GP tremendous. I must say the best GP I've ever [had]. We were with a GP previously and I mentioned it to him several times… he did nothing about it – and then he retired."

"…the response I got was unhelpful and useless. I found the GP to just skim over the whole mental illness thing."

"Well he [GP] kind of dismissed me…the first thing he does was put me on tablets without even talking to me. He kind of started writing while I was talking and just kind of …[here are some] tablets, go away and take them….kind of an attitude like."

"…I appreciated the concern expressed by the GP…but [he] expected me to gain a stone in seven days which terrified me…"

Service users noted that it was difficult to get an appointment at short or relatively short notice even when they were at risk of self-harm.

> "I was very bad at the time. If I wanted to see [a psychiatrist] this was May and I'd have to wait 'til August. And then at August they said to wait another month…"

> "At this stage now like I had lost about two stone in three weeks and I hadn't slept in five days, you know, so I said I need to see someone today if possible. He [GP] said there was no way that's possible…"

> "I would go down to Emergency and sit in Emergency and wait to see someone to say [to them] I was suicidal and I would wait there for about five or six hours and then eventually I would meet a psychologist or a psychiatrist or anybody who they might be able to find."

> "I requested in February…I didn't see anybody until September or October which is too long…"

Initial contact with psychiatrists was similarly variable in degree of understanding and support offered to the service user.

> "She [consultant psychiatrist] was very good. She was full of empathy and I found her to be effective on a therapeutic level anyway. She discussed with me properly the anti-depressants …I felt for the first time in my life there was a glimmer at the end of the tunnel."

> "[Psychiatrist in A & E] spent an hour with me. She was very good …[She said I was] having panic attacks and the only thing for this is medication. Probably counselling as well but medication to begin with. This was 2 a.m. She told me it is not uncommon. She was very good."

> "….[Psychiatrist] didn't help me much at all. She thought that I was just not really copped on, or she though I wasn't really with it d'you know? She was very kind of sarcastic, you know."

> "[Named consultant] who told me to eat more, but even if I didn't it wouldn't matter because someday I would be rushed to hospital anyway." {The thrust of the consultation was pressurising a service user with eating disorder into recovery by implying that she would die if she did begin to eat}.

Thirty four persons (71%) of 'Independent' service users had inpatient experience and 12 (25%) had received treatment through outpatient services of one kind or another. It was un-clear whether two participants who were currently receiving outpatient services had ever received inpatient care. Admission to inpatient care was voluntary for 23 persons (68% of participants who had inpatient care). Eleven service users (32% of those receiving inpatient care) had been admitted involuntarily.

Persons admitted involuntarily noted that this was because they had attempted to harm themselves or were on 'an emotional high'. Two interviewees recalled their experience of admission as very negative.

> "Like everything was out of my control…I was terrified – I was terrified of the place like…"

The other interviewee expressed similar feelings but did not wish these to be recorded verbatim.

A third respondent was upset by witnessing the admission of another service user.

> "…about three security guards restraining [service user who was being admitted] on the ground while [the person] getting an injection."

The other respondents had only a hazy recollection of the event but it did not appear to be negative.

Towards Changing Practice in Initial Consultation and Admission

All GPs should be advised of the importance of responding in a constructive and supportive way to service users who are experiencing psychological/psychiatric problems.

The nature of eating distress as experienced by service users needs to be more thoroughly understood by all medical professionals and they need to be better informed about the most effective interventions available.

Services need to be organised to enable them to respond quickly to the needs of persons who are in crisis, some of whom may be at risk of self-injury or suicide.

Access to state funded mental health services must be made easier and more direct.

Admission practice should be as stress-free and un-traumatic as possible.

Topic 2 Treatment and Therapy

Medication was the dominant form of treatment. Service users had balanced views on the use of drug therapy, seeing it as often useful and sometimes a necessity, but emphasising that it should not be the only or automatically preferred and long- term treatment option.

> "I know medicine keeps you calm and helps you to stay in control and that. But its not so good that you just get tablets 'Take these….' It [the approach to treatment] could be a bit more helpful you know….you are not actually dealing with it [the situation giving rise to the distress] you know…"

> "Its not like I don't appreciate being able to have the wonder anti-depressant drug…It has put quality into my life and I do think it has saved my life. However I'm still sick…I honestly feel the last three – four years haven't been used effectively to bring me more in the clear from depression….The actual happenings in my life have to be recognised and taken into account. [The mental health professionals are] not taking them into account as having anything to do with my illness."

> " I felt that I was being put on tablets too quickly but then again they did help me through a patch….I never really dealt with anything after that [beginning drug treatment] because the tablets were numbing it."

The limited availability of psychological therapies was noted as a deficiency in the publicly funded mental health service. Services users had to arrange and fund this for themselves in many instances.

> " [There should be] more analysing of the patient before putting them on tablets…there's a lot of people who just need to talk…"

> "I want to live my life, I don't want to escape from this life. I want to deal with what's going on here and then get over it and move on…That's what I feel is lacking in this system – the psychiatric system. I feel there's a severe lack in the whole counselling area…I do feel there's a lack of looking at the whole picture. Its not just symptoms and chemicals. Its what has occurred in a person's life – [its not just] what you present with."

> "Psychology [therapy] [was] interesting and effective at first but then the appointments became more infrequent…[with the result that] the therapy got disjointed and messy…"

> "I had to go private. There was too long to wait [to access psychological therapy through the health system]."

> "Its an awful shame that you have to go private. God forbid if a person can't afford to be private."

One respondent felt strongly that psychotherapy sessions should be kept more confidential than is currently the case.

> "You should be able to have private ideas. Really confidential and private counselling. More personal thoughts should be private [between therapist and client] unless the person allowed it...You need to have your own [strictly private] space to let things out." {This service user arranged to have counselling privately rather than through the mental health service to ensure this level of privacy and confidentiality}.

A majority of service users who were offered counselling/psychotherapy found it beneficial.

> "The psychologist is great and knows what is in my head. I used to see [psychologist] once a week but now it is down to once a month."

> "I have cognitive behaviour therapy every three-four weeks. It is a good help."

> "...the counsellor [is] the best person I've seen. The counsellor is fantastic I don't think I would have got through it without her..."

> "I done anxiety management which I found absolutely fantastic. What was great about that was the fact that I met people who were the exact same as me. Because even my counsellor said – she's qualified, but she's never 'been there'." {Never experienced anxiety in the way the speaker has}.

> "I got into this panic management programme [at Health Centre]...I asked about it and they put me in it. I'd be lost without it...without them – the multi-disciplinary team. Even my sisters can see the change."

A number of service users rejected the 'talking therapies' or found them difficult to engage with or found them unsuitable.

> "I could have got counselling but I didn't want it."

> "I found it hard to put into words what I was feeling."

> "I went to a counsellor for a few weeks. I paid for it myself [but] I did not find it helpful."

The emphasis on behavioural interventions and medication in the treatment of eating distress within the publicly funded (and in some cases private) mental health system was noted to be ineffective.

> " [psychiatrist] was very pleasant and caring but his focus was on the behaviour…the focus was on behaviour around food – not on me as a person. I believe that food was my coping mechanism and when I did improve regarding binges/vomiting etc., I actually became very depressed…". {Service user suggests that her eating distress was diverting attention from an underlying problem and she began to achieve a sustained recovery when this was dealt with through the more holistic therapeutic approach of a private specialist psychotherapy service}.

And service users with this problem generally found the enforced bed reset and compulsory eating and reward-punishment modus operandi of the treatment offensive and upsetting.

> "…I was confined to bed and privileges normally allowed to be enjoyed by others [service users] were taken from me...the system was based on the traditional force feeding model...although a television was within earshot - distance I wasn't allowed to watch it. The whole experience was a punishing model."

The point of activities carried out under the label of 'occupational therapy' was not always clear to mental health service users in general.

> "There is so-called meditation. A person walks in with a tape and plays it and then they walk out again…You just feel very demeaned, put down. You need encouragement. The games are ok but…[service user felt the activities were random and without a clear purpose]."

> "OT…it was quite pleasant but it was more or less a way of passing the day. I couldn't see the point of it really."

> "Cutting up paper; reading the paper; talking about the events of the day…"? {Interviewee did not find these activities stimulating or helpful}.

Consultants who actively managed medication by modifying a dose, changing a drug, and/or attempting to deal with side effects in consultation with service users were rated highly.

> "I found him [consultant] friendly and he wasn't threatening…He was fair and I found him good - trustworthy like….I've built up a trust with my own psychiatrist. He is somebody that I can confide in and I do trust. I don't fear him like [I did] the other fella" [Another consultant].

> "Dr [consultant's name]…he's quite young and I think very receptive…he didn't make a big deal about it [service user's refusal of a particular drug]…the fact that I was willing to go on one of the mood stabilisers…I think that he felt we could work together."

> "Dr [consultant's name] is my doctor at the moment and he's a brilliant doctor. I'd like to compliment him at this point. He's very good. He gives me a chance to talk."

A number of consultants were noted to be reluctant or unwilling to discuss medication and its possible side effects.

> "…about medication and side-effects and that…I feel that they [consultants] don't like to tell you too much, maybe in case you're not going to take the medication…"

> "…I had to go out and borrow a book…to look up particular medication I was on… The side effects weren't properly explained at all… I would have preferred if they wrote down one or two points to remember…the doctors say 'You are not to get carried away thinking about the side-effects all the time…'"

Service users felt that the impact of medication on some aspects of their quality of life were not sufficiently appreciated by their clinicians.

> "The side effects were so sickening and I was trying to hold down a job and I felt completely out of it. I didn't want to stay on them."

> "I've put on loads of weight, and I want something done [about weight]…"

> "…it was a terrible, terrible nine months. The medication wasn't right [so] I was not myself…I stated many times that I was not happy with the medication …and they just said 'Give it time'".

> "…{speaker wants medication changed to reduce unpleasant side effects}…[but] they want to leave well enough alone."

A minority of service users gave examples of clinicians making poor treatment decisions or not noticing/reacting to treatment-related signs. (It is not always clear whether these clinicians were consultants or NCHDs).

> "My [GP] noticed me straight away, as soon as I walked in the door, and he said 'You're on something' [medication] and it was making my mouth go – you know – clinching kind of [interviewee demonstrates]. 'twas swelling my face and stuff and he said 'You have to come off that straight away, you're not taking that anymore" so he just took me off it. And they [staff] never copped it here [in day centre]…they didn't cop the side effects."

> "One of the trainee doctors [NCHDs] put me up to 5mg whereas I should only have 2. He said 'What do you think I should do? and I said 'You should increase my med. because I am not feeling well'…I just thought if you increase medication you feel better…I didn't realise the side effects would be so strong…The doctor didn't even give me [named drug] anti-dote for side effects."

> "The doctor at the Centre took me off all medication and I got very depressed again…"

Lack of continuity of care in both the medical and psychological areas was identified as a problem by participants.

> "I was very happy with her [trainee psychologist]. You couldn't get a nicer woman. [But] you just get to know her and she's gone. That's a bit of a downer."

> "I have had loads of doctors…you get different doctors at the [six monthly] change over. They [new arrivals] wouldn't have a clue about you and I have got [been given] tablets that didn't suit me…"

> "They think because you are being seen by someone you are being looked after." {Interviewee is making the point that therapists are not easily inter-changeable because the relationship between the service user and the professionals is an important part of the treatment}.

> "…a trainee clinical psychologist…she was very good. She was very young but she really was good and effective. I was sorry to see her go…"

> "And if you happen to get someone [NCHD] who has an interest [in eating distress] they would be moving on again in a few months time…".

Choice of therapist and/or key worker (CPN; staff nurse; social worker) should be possible when necessary.

> "There can be a personality clash. I felt she [clinical psychologist] wasn't really interested in my mental illness."

> "That one-to-one nursing [key worker concept]...I found that brilliant. But you're in a right heap if you don't get on with the person!"

Towards Changing Practice in Treatment and Therapy

Consultants who actively manage pharmacological treatment in partnership with individual service users are highly thought of and appreciated. This mode of practice should be the norm in all clinical settings.

Consultants who take service user's ongoing life situation into account and discuss it with them are again deemed to offer a very satisfactory service. This aspect of practice should become the norm.

Procedures for prescribing and monitoring pharmacological treatment must be uniform across the service and must be operated to the highest standard. Regular review of practice in this regard must be ensured and never compromised on.

The absence of non-pharmacological treatment options delivered by appropriately trained professional psychologists, psychotherapists and counsellors and as part of a planned therapeutic structure must be redressed.

The behaviour modification reward-punishment model of treatment offered to some service users with eating distress should be replaced by a more holistic person-centred approach.

The range of non-pharmacological interventions must go beyond the 'talking' psychological therapies to cater for the needs of service users who might find it easier to conceptualise and express their problem through other modes,(e.g., art, drama, music).

Choice of therapist should be possible, and easy to achieve when necessary.

Topic 3 Inpatient Experience

Relationship with Mental Health Professionals

The relationship of clinicians with the service users in their care in the in- patient setting reflected the different styles of engagement or distance described under Topic 2. (Topic 2 covers service user experience of treatment across all service settings).

> "A fair bit of one-to-one [discussion] with the consultant. The consultant was very much on the case I must say."

> "…I found him [psychiatrist] very abrupt and very aggressive. He's a very 'yes' and 'no' man, now you know…there's lots of times he'd kind of cut me off and say 'That's something you should be dealing with [with psychologist]. I'm asking you a question now so can you just give me a 'yes' or a 'no'? just answer exactly'…"

> "…you get close to doctors and you get close to nurses and they're my friends and without them I wouldn't be alive."

> "The doctor [would say] 'Do you have any stupid thoughts? I thought that was kind of degrading – if he said 'Do you have any 'down' thoughts – I feel sometimes some of the psychiatrists…there are just so many people maybe they can't be empathetic like – but you felt you were a piece of meat."

More frequent rounds by clinicians would be desirable.

> "Doctors normally see you on Monday or Friday. And I would suggest that they try and see patients more… if they could at all you know. They're not able to see you, they haven't got the time…but it is needed, it is needed. It's the doctor you want to see…"

The team meeting was singled out as a particularly negative and unhelpful aspect of the relationship of health professionals with users of their service.

> {This interviewee noted that 1 of these meetings was held each week. Only the consultant spoke at these meetings} "I have to say these meetings were daunting. Everybody else [other team members] just sat there…I was crying, crying, crying and I just wanted somebody to hold my hand…I knew they all felt for me [but nobody consoled the service user]. What were these people here for?…I do feel it would be nicer if they all had a little bit of input."

> "They brought me into a room with about eight other people…I think I knew two of them. And they were just sitting around in a circle and I felt so…stupid… I don't even know their names. I don't know who they are but they know about me! That gets to me…They were all talking among themselves… [but not to service user]."

Nurses were generally rated highly...

> "Excellent staff, I must admit like you couldn't ask for better. But they are kind of short staffed every now and then."

> "There was...more than a few nurses that were really helpful, you know?

> "...the whole the nursing staff, I really couldn't fault them...the majority they're just angels...and they want to help you."

Although their job structure was experienced as disruptive of the service users' connection with nursing staff.

> "You had a different nurse every day so it was quite confusing...maybe if they could just concentrate on one nurse to a patient for their time there rather than changing every day..."

> "....and the staff haven't got time to give them [service users] a bit more sort of treatment, you know what I mean. They haven't got time for that ...or else they would I'm sure. But its [nursing staff therapy with service users], definitely needed."

> "I do feel there should be administrative staff...[to allow nurses time to work therapeutically with service users]..."

And a minority of nursing staff were considered to be unsupportive and to have a custodial and generally unpleasant attitude to those in their care.

> "There was a nurse...he started making derogatory remarks and he was very dogmatic towards me..."

> " I was afraid of the dark, right, and they wouldn't let me sleep with the light on. I felt I was being treated like an animal [by night staff]..."

> "...some [nursing staff] were intimidating. You wouldn't know whether you could trust them with yourself or not, you know."

> "...she was very abrupt and mean, I thought."

Nursing care was experienced as particularly poor by persons experiencing eating distress.

> "[Service user was admitted at lunch time and did not feel like eating]…The ward sister said, 'You're going to have to learn to eat sometime, you know."

> "Most [nursing staff] acted as if we had brought our illness on ourselves or were looking for attention. Many instances of self-harm by others or [by] myself were met with contempt and confusion. Instead of trying to understand or discover why it was done, they…just bandaged up a wound or sent for x-ray, then continued on as normal."

A service user who had experienced more regular contact with nursing staff noted how good this can be.

> "…where there might be three nurses on different shifts that might be assigned to you; I found that fantastic because you're going to the same person all the time with the problem. You build up a relationship."

Special Problems with the Inpatient Setting

One respondent had experienced seclusion and/or restraint and one had experienced pressure to comply with medication. Three service users mentioned their distress at witnessing another service user being restrained or put in seclusion.

> "I was put on anti-psychotics" {Speaker felt compelled to accept the medication}.

> "…it was a terrible experience…they put me in a cell, like a prison… they needed to confine me because [of speaker's psychological state]."

> "Like I seen a fellow being thrown into a room. He tried to get out you know. He panicked and he was charging toward the doors [of the ward] and he was opening doors and everything else. They stuck a needle in him and stuck him in a room and monitored him…"

> "A young boy aged 14 or 15 pinned up against a wall while wearing a bed sheet…"

Daily Life in the Inpatient Facility

Planned therapeutic activities were generally absent...

> "I spent most of my days walking the corridors."

> "There were different activities...but for most of the time you were just idle. Just sitting around talking, watching the television or something like that."

Although one facility had a very well-structured and vibrant programme.

> "Well there was plenty to do there...There was lots of different courses – you could paint, [take] woodwork classes...all sorts of different things [were] going on."

Weekends were mentioned as a particularly difficult time, when even the more random Occuptional Therapy activities were not available. (The more structured programme was also not available at weekends).

> "At weekends there was no OT which made the weekends very long. Everybody just dreaded Saturday and Sunday, particularly if they didn't have regular visitors."

> "...during the weekends they'd all – all that kind of staff [OTs] just goes home and your left with nothing but the TV and there's nothing on TV [at] weekends anyway."

The Physical and Psychological Environment

Décor was noted as being drab and the setting had an 'institutional' feel about it.

> "The day room would be kind of a depressing place...its not bright enough."

> "The nurses make an effort to make the place not institutionalised-looking. They rearranged the furniture you know, so that you could be sitting in a kind of a circle maybe..."

The absence of quiet rooms for those who wished not to watch TV or be constantly in the presence of others was noted.

> "[In the day room] people are in your face all the time."

> "...need a library area [where you can read in quietness]."

The availability of tea or coffee outside set times, especially for one's visitors, would make the setting less institution-like.

> "An area where you could have access to tea or coffee – even if it was only a vending machine. With your visitors ..."

The need for physical exercise was noted.

> "...a sports hall or something...where you could, you know, play basket ball, play indoor soccer or something like that..."

> "There is space for a garden there. It would be good to do a bit of gardening."

> "One of the nurses is trying to set up a garden...[she is] trying to do this on her own. It would be very helpful."

Although understanding why it might be necessary, many service users felt uneasy about being under constant or near-constant surveillance and felt their personal dignity was undermined by having to wear night clothes and be accompanied when showering.

> "The only thing I didn't like is that we were locked in and you had to ask for 'parole' they called it – it was a funny word for being allowed out....like it was a prison or something."

> "The only place where you had some privacy was the smoking room because you had no camera there....That place isn't very healthy. They did try to ventilate but there's green moss collecting on the windows! Its not a pleasant place to be!"

> "I didn't like my clothes being taken from me."

> "You know a simple thing like going for a shower, you'd have to take up your nurse [with you]..."

The lack of privacy when entertaining visitors was also noted.

> "If you had a visitor [they must be entertained in the day room or dormitory with other service users present] ...some people [service users] don't know not to invade your space...one or two private areas would be good and there is nothing for children to play with if they come in to visit you."

All participants who had inpatient experience remarked on the need to allow for the different requirements of service users depending upon their psychological state and their progress towards recovery.

> "Maybe the wards could do with more segregation…we're all different, mixed abilities. And although I can see the advantages of keeping everybody together…I can see disadvantages to the patient who may be depressed and who may therefore become more depressed…"

> "It was scary. What I didn't like is that you had addicts beside people with depression. There should be different areas. If it's a psychiatric ward you shouldn't put people who are detoxing from drugs or alcohol in with people with mental illness."

> "There was this one person and he used to talk to himself – day in, day out. And it used to drive me nuts. Your need to be in a reasonably peaceful place."

> "When I went in there people were very kind of sedated looking, you know. That was a bit off-putting…when they're sedated and don't know what is going on."

Towards Changing Practice in the Inpatient Service

Advances in the delivery of inpatient care would include:

Greater availability of medical professional staff to discuss and work with service users, and a lessening of administrative demands on these staff through assigning such work to administrative personnel.

Availability of non-pharmacological therapies of a variety of kinds (e.g., art, music, drama, as well as the 'talking therapies' to meet the variety of needs of the full range of service users.

Enhancing skills of nurse specialists in working with service users experiencing eating distress in other than a punitive mode.

Availability of a professionally designed and delivered comprehensive occupational therapy programme that would be graded to the changing needs of service users, and which would be available at weekends as well as weekdays.

Review of layout and design to create a less institutional setting, with smaller spaces to cater for service users needs for tranquillity, and for privacy when entertaining visitors.

Availability of recreational spaces for physical activity such as a sports or garden etc.

As noted in Section 3, examination of the research literature and consultation with service users and mental health service providers and professionals (in Ireland and elsewhere) to determine more satisfactory ways of dealing with acceptance of treatment, extreme service user distress, and security while minimising the intrusion on users' privacy and personal dignity through surveillance and not being allowed to wear day clothes.

The policy and practice of having persons with mixed psychological needs and at different stages of recovery in the same location should be re-considered by service providers. The views of service users on how current arrangements affect their recovery should form an important element in this review.

Topic 4 Discharge Procedure

Interviewees with inpatient experience did not comment on the administrative aspect of their discharge.

Psychological preparation for discharge and immediate support after leaving the Inpatient facility was variable.

> "You're going out of hospital where there's loads of people and then you come into a room [at home] and there's nobody there…and you feel isolated. After I left hospital… a home visit, some support at home, would have been nice."

> "[Consultant] talked to me and said I'd be taking the tablets for a year…[and to] take it easy for the first few days [at home]. Then try to find something – a course or something. The CPN called once a week for the first month. I did a FÁS course [CPN helped to arrange it]."

> "I had great support from my social worker and my consultant…"

> "Nobody prepares you for when you are asked out or people come in and you have to deal with food…A lot of life – in your family and social life – is around food…Nobody prepares you to deal with that…"{Comment from person experiencing eating distress}.

Family members may need support when the service user returns home and this is not a routine part of the mental health service in all catchment areas at this time.

> "My children didn't know what was going on."

> "[Spouse]…wasn't happy with the way she was treated as regards finding out information about me…she was told not to worry, that I 'would be sorted out'. She was a bit upset about that."

Towards Changing Practice in Discharge Procedure

Preparation for discharge through discussion of service users concerns by consultant, CPN, or social worker, with arrangements for an appropriate immediate contact (e.g., home visit or 'phone call).

Preparation of family members for service users' return home. The approach needs to be sensitive to the needs of children as well as adults.

A note to the Reader on Topics 5/6 Experience of Day hospital/Day Centre Services

The terms day hospital and day centre were not clearly distinguishable from these interviews. A number of interviewees used the terms interchangeably within the same sentence and respondents generally did not make a distinction between the settings in terms of their assessment of the service received. Consequently the information on both is presented under a single composite heading – **Experience of Day Care**

Topics 5 /6   Experience of Day Care and Ancillary Community Services

Interviewees felt that day care was available to them if they wished to avail of it. It serves a mainly social support function for these service users.

> "I could go to classes in the day centre if I wanted to but I don't need them because I work and I have a family and a grandchild."

> "I go to the centre and meet people, and sometimes [I] go to the classes and the quizzes. The staff are great support."

> "…because you've always got someone to talk to…you feel you're not alone."

> "[Named day centre]…you can go in if you need someone to talk to. They are really great. I couldn't imagine them turning anybody away…"

The NDTI was singled out as offering a good service to those seeking training with a view to employment.

> " The NDTI were very good. They are very sound."

Community care by the CPN and social work services was much appreciated but was not as available as much as some service users needed. This was particularly so where service users could not easily access day care.

> "[CPN] comes out here maybe once or twice a month. To see how things are doing, to have a chat, to talk about whatever need that I might have."

> "I think it would be nice…to have had a follow-up service after I left the hospital…to begin with, you know."

> "I feel I'm not getting enough support. I have a good doctor and…I'm lucky to have a consultant…but I feel I'm not getting enough support. Its not enough just to see the doctor maybe every couple of months or six weeks you know."

Towards Changing Practice in Day Care and Ancillary Community Services

Accessibility is an important aspect of the day care service, which is otherwise deemed to offer good social support to service users.

Home visits are an important element in assuring quality care for service users who cannot access day care centres. Visits are particularly important when a service user first returns from inpatient care.

Topic 7 Outpatient Experience

The brief consultation time and the lack of continuity of care were cited by the majority of interviewees as negative and worrying features of the outpatient experience.

> " [consultation is]…about 10 minutes…"

> "It was go in, get your medication, say how you are, say if you have any side effects and back out again…"

> "In three – four years I've seen about twenty different psychiatrists and two actually listened to me and had read my notes and actually made suggestions that were therapeutic…they were…in a hurry, under pressure and I felt I shouldn't take up much of their time. That wasn't seeing a psychiatrist…that was seeing an administrator! You feel sorry for them – sorry for that person at the other side of the table. I felt like I needed to cheer them up! Very despondent, un-responsive psychiatrists administering drugs."

> "…it's a bit worrying if you're meeting different people every time you go in…you just fear what they might do…you might get someone who might want to go off on a totally different track…"

> "…You were just getting to know a doctor and they'd move on. They'd change every six months …you've told everything to her and then you'd come along the next day and a totally different doctor [is there] and they wouldn't have a clue [about your problems]."

More assertive and confident service users insisted on seeing their consultant.

> "They [others service users] say 'No' to the trainees. They say 'I am waiting for the consultant."

> "I only want to see the consultant. I'm not explaining my story all over again to another doctor…why should I have to go through that every time?"

Excessively long waiting periods and the lack of confidentiality when there are multiple appointments for the same time was noted.

> "You could be waiting two hours…three hours."

> "I think you should have a certain time [for an appointment]…The way you all meet in the waiting room – I wouldn't like people knowing my business…I'd prefer if we had all different times."

Topic 8 The Treatment Plan

In the absence of a comprehensive range of interventions treatment planning could only refer to service users use of medication. The extent to which this intervention was planned and discussed with the service users reflected the consultant's usual style of relating to service users. Thus some explained their thinking on the drug regime to their clients while others did not.

Topic 9 Service Users' Rights and Advocacy

This was mentioned by one service user.

This interviewee did not wish to be taped. The service user became an inpatient voluntarily, but was then changed to an involuntary admission when certified by two GPs. " They certified me without speaking to me. I was treated worse than a criminal."

Towards Changing Practice in Service Users' Rights and Advocacy

The comments made on this topic in Section 4 apply here.

Section 6

Diversity of Need Across the Mental Health Spectrum: Implications for Service Design, Quality and Delivery

Section 6

Diversity of Need Across the Mental Health Spectrum: Implications for Service Design, Quality and Delivery

6.1.0 Introduction

6.1.1   In the course of this project we were struck by the heterogeneity of needs and experiences that the classification 'mental illness' embraces and perhaps conceals. This factor emerged most clearly when participants were speaking about the inpatient and day hospital services. In this section we look at the various issues investigated from the point of view of people experiencing particular types of mental health problems and note the service needs that they have arising from their specific difficulty.

6.2.0 The Views of Persons Experiencing Disordered Cognition

6.2.1   Persons experiencing disordered cognition may be unable to differentiate the inner dialogue that we all carry on with ourselves as we go about our lives from speech originating in the world around them. A person may therefore say that they are 'hearing voices' that are saying unpleasant or critical things, when in fact it is his/her own inner commentary or personal fantasy that is going on. Some people may misinterpret what they hear or see because they have difficulty in focusing or maintaining attention in the way others do. Consequently they may feel a person or situation is threatening when most people would see it as benign.

6.2.2   Service users with these experiences needed the option of a quiet environment with less information overload.

"There was lots of people around. And the television would be on all day which I found irritating. I used to try to get away [from the noise]… I would ask the nurse…Maybe sometimes a good nurse…would let me into the library or the art room…I would go away for a quiet place."

" I didn't know if it was the TV…if it was other people…or on the TV… or my voices…"

They also needed to feel psychologically safer than some circumstances allowed.

"I found it quite distressing at the time that sometimes police would drop different inpatients into the clinic and the story would go around that this fellow stabbed someone down town or something like that, and it'd make you sleep very uneasy."

"…there was this one woman I used to be afraid of her; and in the end she attacked me a few times."

"There was another guy that used to walk around naked in the ward …and he could be coming right up beside your bed – stone naked – and he would just stand there like…he was just standing there like with fear in his eyes…he was harmless, but at the same time…" [service user felt confused and threatened].

6.3.0   The Views of Persons Experiencing Extreme Anxiety

6.3.1   Persons experiencing extreme levels of anxiety often had difficulties accessing available services because of the nature of their problem.

{Service user explained that the dread that was part of the condition prevented actually getting help to overcome it} "…I remember having appointments with the psychiatrist and I couldn't go them…"

"…I used to be crying and getting attacks all the way up the road [to see a counsellor]."

{Service user noted that people with the problem may be unable to get to the mutual help group to avail of its self-help programme} "…people couldn't get out to go to the [group] meeting."

The layout of the inpatient facility could exacerbate service users' anxiety.

"What killed me altogether was with the panic attacks I couldn't cope with people around me, or people behind me. I was put into a ward with six people so I would be in bed at night and oh! like that [service user demonstrates gasping for air] at a window but there would be three others with panic attacks at the same window! God, I mean…that is exactly the way it was."

"If you are frightened to go out of the house never mind say into an environment that we don't even know…"

"…there were people in the ward that did sing and that did shout. Great people - some of them turned out to be my best friends – but when you walk in and someone is singing and shouting…they frightened me."

6.4.0   The Views of Persons Experiencing Disorders of Mood

6.4.1   Disordered mood can involve swings between elation and deep sadness and feelings of hopelessness, or they can involve sadness and hopelessness only. People in general will experience mood changes from time to time in different circumstances. Persons for whom these changes persist and may be excessive in degree and/or duration for the circumstance that gave rise to them, experience much distress and suffering.

6.4.2   An interviewee who had experienced elation noted wryly that during these phases they thought everything about the services was excellent.

"I thought it was all grand. I was high at the time you know…maybe that's why I thought it was grand!"

Individual differences in temperament seems to play a part in the experience of elated people when in the inpatient setting.

"For the first few days everything irritated me…I couldn't handle it. Noise and everything."

6.4.3   Persons experiencing depressed mood found that once they themselves began to recover, being with others who felt depressed or who were troubled and distressed in other ways slowed their own progress.

" There's no streaming of patients, you know. I could be well and I'm among… patients who are not well."

6.5.0   The Views of Persons Experiencing Eating Disorder

6.5.1   The structure of inpatient services does not suit the needs of persons suffering from eating distress. The following aspects of service structure are particularly unsuited to the needs of this group of service users.

○ Set meal times – which diminishes service users' sense of control.

○ Communal eating.

○ Limited or no choice of menu.

○ Presentation of the food in ways that may not be enticing.

6.6.0   Implications of Diversity for Service Design, Quality, and Delivery

6.6.1   We do not know whether this diversity of needs is recognised in principle by the mental health services. If it is recognised, it is evident that it is not catered for by the way in which the inpatient and some day hospital services are structured/organised.

6.6.2   The absence of a service model which is sensitive to the diverse needs of service users along the lines outlined in paragraphs **6.2.1** through **6.4.1** inevitably affects the quality of the therapy offered to clients.

6.6.3   Large dormitory-type sleeping accommodation is unsuitable for most service users. Such spaces lack privacy. They will appear frightening and/or uncontrollable to service users who feel threatened in large public spaces or by the presence of many others. Large day rooms will have a similar effect.

6.6.4   Communal dining is not suited to the needs of all service users. This is especially so for persons experiencing eating distress. Service users generally who are further along the path to recovery may find dining with others whose table manners have deteriorated because of their current psychological state off-putting and upsetting. Arrangements to facilitate these differences are a necessary part of a therapeutic environment.

6.6.5   The constant presence of others, the 'always on' TV or radio, and the absence of smaller more home-like quiet rooms, which are pleasantly decorated, in which to read, study, chat, play board games, and entertain ones visitors, as well as the absence of an exercise area for physical activity, all reduce the therapeutic potential of the inpatient and similar settings.

Section 7
Findings from the Carers' Focus Group

Section 7

Findings from the Carers' Focus Group

7.1.0   Introduction

7.7.1 The eighth focus group was composed of carers of service users. The findings from that group are considered here. Seven persons, three women and four men, took part in this group. All were members of the carer section of an organisation for persons experiencing severe and often enduring psychological disorder.

Topic 1 Initial Contact with the Mental Health Services

Carers' initial contact with the publicly funded mental health service generally occurred through the family GP. The members of this group highlighted families' dependence on their GP for information and guidance.

> "…he [GP] was the guy you depend on to take you seriously."

> "…to get a section you have to get your GP's support. For your GP to make a diagnosis you have to get the patient to the GP. How do you get somebody who thinks there's nothing wrong with them to the GP?…he [GP] listened to me. I was lucky with my GP. Very, very [lucky]…I had GP support, number one. Without which you're nowhere because that person [family member] was over age."

They remarked on the variation in quality of the knowledge and communication skills of GPs.

> "We would have mixed views about how adequate he [GP] was in the whole situation…he diagnosed…but didn't give us any what we regarded as useful advice on how to cope with it. No information. No advice. Well, our GP's advice was you know, 'Make [family member] face up to reality', you know, 'push him out on his own and leave him there', you know? Which we didn't do thankfully…as the illness got more severe and acute…"

> {Speaking about the need for the GP to be able to explain the problem in 'lay persons' language' a carer said} "Because being told that you have schizophrenia or that your family member has it doesn't advance anything."

> "[named GP] he was absolutely wonderful. His diagnosis to me was that [family member] had a thought disorder." {This practitioner then explained 'thought disorder' to the carer in terms of how it affected the behaviour of the service user}.

The very difficult decision to seek the involuntary admission of a family member is compounded by the lack of a standard procedure to allow this to be done efficiently and sensitively.

> "…the worst thing I ever had to do in my entire life [was arrange an involuntary admission]. I had to get a little thing from the doctor saying that 'Yes' [family

member should be admitted]. Then I had to call the police. There was nobody. I was alone. I had to go and knock on my [family member's] door and get him to come with me to the hospital…The Judas at the door. You are waiting maybe 2-3 hours to see a consultant…and it being the way it is [shortage of beds] they will not admit somebody unless they feel it's [essential]. So I was praying he would be as crazy as possible in front of the doctor!…you can imagine being disloyal [to your family member] and nobody from the Social Services there in any shape or form to support you."

"…two members of [nursing] staff physically held [family member] down…to forcefully give him medication. And [family member] is quite a docile guy…. That was shocking. That actually worsened his condition. He was already bad but that tipped him completely. We were horrified. And I had signed the papers…[for admission]."

Professionals need to be sensitive to the impact their words can have on carers, especially on first contact.

"The first time I actually got [family member] up in [named psychiatric facility] the consultant told me what the diagnosis was and said, 'I think I would rather be telling you that [family member] has AIDS. And [that] was a top consultant!"

Towards Changing Practice in Initial Contact and Admission From the Carer Perspective

Giving relevant and practical information and guidance to carers and to do it in a sensitive way is a core skill for GPs and mental health professionals.

Family members should not be expected to be the sole organisers of an involuntary admission. Admitting staff should be aware of their feelings of fear, anxiety and perhaps guilt, and should offer support during and immediately following the admission procedure.

Topic 2 Treatment and Therapy

Carers noted that non-pharmacological therapies often had to be arranged and paid for privately.

> "We won't get it [counselling] because it – they decided that it is not appropriate, that [service user] won't respond to it…we are doing it privately now. But through the services we are being denied completely."

> "There is [counselling] but we can't get it."

The role of the consultant as 'gate-keeper' to accessing the services of allied mental health professionals was also described.

> "If you want to see the psychologist who is working on the therapy – behavioural side with your child on the outpatient or when they are in hospital, you have to first go through…the consultant and ask [their] permission because if you go direct to [psychologist] then it is all politics. So you have to get [consultant] to say, 'Yes, it is O.K. for you to speak to [psychologist].' Or else he [psychologist] gets into trouble and stuff."

Carers noted the unwillingness of psychiatrists to work towards reducing service users' dependence on medication. GPs willing to work in partnership with the service user and the carer(s) on reducing medication were commended by carers who had worked in this way with their family GP.

> "[Professionals say there is] 'no cure!' But then you have people like my [family member] who has chosen to come off the medication. He is still a schizophrenic. He still has his thoughts. He still has his moments. But he has got to a stage through – with me helping him, he could actually live alone."

> "…we went to [consult another doctor] and he advised us to start weaning her off the drug…we did get to .5mg…[dose] had been 6. And then we noticed that [the] paranoia started coming back, so we upped it half a milligram for a few months and [service user] was grand…and we put it down half a milligram. We stopped going to the clinic because the psychiatrist wouldn't support that. So now we just keep a careful eye on things – ourselves and the GP."

Towards Changing Practice in Treatment and Therapy

Carers should be able to access professionals from all of the mental health disciplines for consultation directly and without undue delay.

Medication should be part of a broader package of interventions.

The possibility of reducing or otherwise modifying pharmacological treatments in co-operation with carers should be seriously considered.

Topic 3 Experience of the Inpatient Service

Relationship with Mental Health Professionals.

Carers noted that their knowledge of the service user was seldom if ever sought by mental health professionals; that their enquiries were rebuffed; and that the prevailing approach was to actively exclude them from the care of their family member. Yet they were often the persons on whom the service user depended most when not an inpatient.

> "The problem is that they [mental health professionals] don't listen to the parents and relatives sufficiently. They completely underestimate the value of the relative's appraisal of the situation. Even though it may be a lay appraisal, it is a very intimate knowledge that they possess. And these guys [professionals] tend to…they totally disregard a lot…"

> "I had bought the book and read about the thing [tardive dyskinesia]…I went up to the hospital and said 'Look this [treatment side effect] can be irreversible.' First [consultant] said, 'Oh no, no.' 'Look' I said, 'it is written down there by a doctor.' And he [family member] was taken off it…[medication]."

> "[Named consultant] was dismissive of anything I would say, even about treatment or facilities…[consultant] was not open about anything."

The carers noted considerable variation in the attitudes and behaviours of nursing staff.

> "A lot of the staff – the nursing staff – are excellent. Others behave like jailers."

When in place and fully functioning the multidisciplinary team are recognised as probably being effective but service users noted that

> "...with our medical services in Ireland - they'll talk about multi-disciplinary teams in Ireland but exactly in what way [do] they actually function? Because everything is aspirational in Ireland."

> "All aspirations and no performance!"

Daily Life in the Inpatient Facility

Carers described a lack of recreational activities and facilities for inpatients. Where such facilities did exist, access depended on the supervision and availability of ward staff. Inadequate ventilation in the smoking room was also commented upon.

> "...they have a games room which consists of a table tennis table to which access is denied unless a member of staff volunteers to play table tennis with them."

> "The smoking rooms in there – unbelievable! You don't need to light a cigarette at all, like!"

The Physical and Psychological Environment

Carers spoke of the need for the ward environment to reflect the needs of the service user, especially when the duration of inpatient stay is likely to be lengthy. They were surprised that these needs were often not catered for in the newer acute units.

> "...denied all access to fresh air. Absolutely no exercise facilities of any sort...to be denied access to fresh air is – I think is probably against the European Convention of Human Rights. Or any form of exercise...and it is a brand new facility! We complained about that [lack of exercise] you know, at length and eventually after a lot of complaining – some of the staff now are brilliant – some of them they brought [family member] out and walked him around the block."

> "[Family member] was in the acute unit for much longer than...the unit is designed to cater for... . There is an assumption that you will be there only for a short time. There is no forward thinking and because of that there wasn't a structure [suitable to a longer stay]."

Carers noted that service users do not always feel safe or comfortable in the inpatient setting.

> "…you wake up in the night and an old man looking straight in your face. Or you go to the toilet and come back [and] some old fellow is in your bed or going around in your pyjamas. So if you [are emotionally upset] it is pretty scary."

Maintenance needs to be on-going since shabby and damaged structures undermine one's sense of wellbeing.

> "Three years ago [named facility] had holes in the ceiling, holes in the walls…an unpleasant sort of place to be. I don't know if it's improved any."

Towards Changing Practice in the Inpatient Service

As viewed by carers improved inpatient care would include:

Facilitating service users' right of accessing to fresh air and outdoor spaces.

Easy access to a range of recreational and physical activities.

Ensuring non-intrusion of others into the service user's personal space and ensuring that service users feel safe.

Attention to on-going maintenance of the physical environment.

Topic 4 Discharge Procedure

The discharge procedure was an area of concern for these carers.

> "…[Family member] just rang and told me that he was sitting down in the foyer. Now luckily he has me and I'm there for him. But the number of people that are discharged and just left back into the community. Nobody checks where they are going to – are they on their own?"

> "They [service users] can't do anything for themselves. I think they [service providers] should be obliged when they are discharging somebody from hospital – that they should be discharged to an external professional like the psychiatric social person…who can keep an eye on them. Anything else is utterly – it is irresponsible actually."

Accommodation services for those recently discharged but not yet ready to live with their family were inappropriate for vulnerable service users.

> "[Because of the effect on other family members] we refused to have him home…
> And the resolution was [named hostel] for homeless men was the only
> accommodation they claimed they could find for him… . He rang me in tears, 'There
> are people who are alcoholics, there's people who have just come out of jail,
> criminals. I am afraid in my room.' Like it was absolutely horrific." "[There is] No half-
> way house."

Towards Changing Practice at Discharge

The discharge process should involve:

Preparation of both service user and carer for the service user's discharge on a known date.

The provision of a variety of levels of support from CPNs and social workers which can be matched to service user and carer needs.

The provision of a variety of graded 'step-down' accommodation in the community suitable to the needs of psychologically vulnerable people not yet ready to live at the family home or independently.

Topics 5/6   Day Care and Ancillary Community Services

The problem of 'access' to day hospital and day care facilities was raised.

> "I asked about a day hospital and I was told there is no day hospital suitable for
> your… [family member]."

> "Well in theory you have day hospitals and day centre scattered through any health
> board…but they raise issues about how the service users are going to get the
> places."

> "[Family member] attended…a day hospital placement…where he was given one
> hour a week and he was the only person in the class."

Carers spoke very highly of rehabilitative work schemes offered by the National Training and Development Institute (NTDI) and FÁS, but noted that the time period offered to service users on such schemes was limited.

> "If somebody goes through that [NTDI] they do their time through FÁS where they go into an employer for a certain length of time. The unfortunate thing is…they are there for six months and they are feeling very good about themselves – their self-esteem, their confidence – but the trouble is they only get six months, maximum a year."

> "Community employment jobs…they are good because they are like short hours and they are very good for people with schizophrenia. But they are very insecure."

Towards Changing Practice in the Day hospital/Day Centres and Ancillary Community Services

Day hospitals and centres should offer more places and have well-designed programmes.

The placements through NDTI/FÁS and the SES should be permanent or at least semi-permanent in duration since they are particularly suited to the needs of persons with severe mental illness.

Topic 7 Outpatient Experience

The lack of continuity of care and the long waiting period resulting from the multiple booking appointment system in the outpatient clinic were a source of frustration and concern to carers.

> "We never saw the same doctor twice."

> "Fifty others [service users] all appear at the same time and you are sitting there waiting, waiting, waiting. Eventually it's a two minute job – a jab [injection] and out the door and that's it."

> "Every single time he goes in it takes five minutes [and] it's a different person who reads about him. How can they [monitor service user's progress]?"

Community support from CPNs and social workers would be welcome but was in too short supply.

> "Psychiatric social workers...to help you when the person is ill initially..."

> "And then when they are coming out of hospital again they need daily support and we [carers] badly need support there again..."

Towards Changing Practice in Outpatient Services

Changes in the way in which these services are organised to ensure continuity of care and to minimise waiting times mentioned in the preceding sections also apply here.

Carers should be involved in part of the discussion between the service user and the consultant so as to maximise all available information for the benefit of both the service user and the carer.

Community support through home visits to give information and advice and to suggest strategies that both the carer and service user might find useful should be routinely available independently of whether a crisis or emergency has occurred.

Topic 8 Treatment Plan

Medical professionals were unwilling to engage in a more collaborative process with families in terms of discussing the treatment regimen.

> "...and they [consultants] absolutely refused point blank [to discuss service user's treatment with carer]. Medication, stabilisation and you're grand. No discussion. You're [carer] not entertained."

Towards Changing Practice in Treatment Planning

All remarks already made on desirability of involving carers in service user treatment/therapy apply here.

Topic 9 Service User Right and Advocacy

This matter was not discussed as such by carers. However their concern about the procedure involved in involuntary admissions and their feelings of responsibility around this event (which are acute if their family member was roughly treated) come under this heading.

More generally these carers voiced concern for people who do not have a carer to seek out services for them.

> "And the only people with schizophrenia that avail of these [NTDI/FÁS] courses are people who have carers. The majority of people…they have nobody to – like – no outside force to help them along…"

CODA TO PART II

CHANGES OVER TIME?

It is evident that the publicly funded mental health services require rejuvenation through a sustained systematic programme of adequate, evidence based, and imaginative development across a number of areas. These areas include service content, multi-disciplinary staff recruitment and development, and investment in physical infra-structure, and they are discussed further in Part III. Meanwhile it is should be noted that there are some encouraging signs of change and even more importantly of a readiness to change in the findings set out in the preceding sections. These indicators are outlined next.

EVIDENCE OF CHANGE

Twenty-eight participants had begun to use the publicly funded mental health service within the last three years. Twenty participants were using it for longer than three years, and a number of these participants had been using the services for 20 or more years. Service users experiencing extreme anxiety who have begun to use the mental health service within the last three years (<3 years) appear to be offered therapies such as anxiety management or stress management as well as medication, and these non-pharmacological interventions were delivered in a community setting. These are welcome developments.

Although medication remained the treatment of choice for most clinicians for mood and thought disorders, a minority of service users (coming mainly from the <3 years user group) said they had been offered some choice in their medication. Far fewer of the participants who have been availing of the publicly funded mental health services for longer than three years (3+ years) felt that they had any choice in this regard.

These albeit still tentative moves towards the use of non-pharmacological therapies for anxiety conditions delivered in a community setting, and the move towards more discussion of medication with service users show some readiness to look at a range of interventions and to take a partnership approach to working with service users.

It is important that these developments be highlighted and supported, and that other similar developments be encouraged so that the local initiatives of individuals and groups can become part of the culture throughout the service as a whole.

Part 3
Summary of Findings
Strategic Actions

Part 3

Summary of Findings Strategic Actions

Preamble to Part III

In this final part of this report the main findings from the project are summarised first and brief comments are made on their implications. (The paragraphs on 'Towards Changing Practice' that follow the findings for each topic should be consulted for more detail on the specific actions needed to respond to participants' views of each element of the service).

The findings are then linked to relevant studies in Ireland and elsewhere, and to the broader research literature on clinical practice in mental health care. Observations are made on the general issue of creating a quality state funded mental health service.

The question of realising the changes needed to create a quality service based on 'Towards Changing Practice' in the different topic areas, and meeting the needs of service users as it relates to the remit of the Mental Health Commission under the 2001 Mental Health Act is then considered.

Section 8

Summary of Findings, Observations, and suggested Strategic Actions

Section 8

Summary of Findings, Observations, and suggested Strategic Actions

8.1.0 SUMMARY OF FINDINGS

8.1.1 *On Initial Contact with the Publicly Funded Mental Health Service*

○ Services are difficult to access and service users may avoid or delay contact to a critical degree because of the stigma associated with mental illness. **Every effort must be made to educate the public at large about the nature of mental illness and all organs of communication in society need to be made aware of the role they play in creating and maintaining such stigma,** (Wilson, Nairn, Coverdale, & Panapa, 1999). Such efforts should be based on the scientific knowledge available on the processes involved in social cognition, attitude change and the reduction of prejudice available in the social psychology research literature. Exhortation or PR campaigns will not do[14].

○ Although practitioners vary in their knowledge of the various conditions, many GPs offer an excellent service to their patients and work diligently and enthusiastically with them to promote their wellbeing and recovery. A minority of GPs have a dismissive and less informed attitude to persons' experiencing mental illness and **this needs to be urgently addressed by their professional bodies as well as by the medical training schools.**

○ The majority of persons with mental health difficulties are cared for by and only by their GP. Considering the average time allowed for a consultation and the GPs' generalist rather than specialist training, it is not reasonable to expect GPs to meet service user's needs for a non-pharmacological element to their care. In order to deal with this situation **mental health professionals should be included in the primary care team[15].**

○ Emergency services for those in personal crisis that may result in their self-injury or death by suicide are lacking or gravely deficient. Sooner or later the person in crisis will be unable to tolerate the waiting time of hours to be seen at a clinic or in A & E at an acute general hospital, or the months which many must wait for an appointment with a counsellor or psychotherapist. **Concern about suicide and its prevention must be backed up by accessible and fast-responding services on the ground.**

---

14   *The insights and experience of groups in the mental health field such as Mental Health Ireland and the service user mutual help organisations could also be drawn upon.*

15   *This does not mean that there must be a psychiatrist, psychologist, and social worker etc. in each practice. A team of such people could service multiple practices with some professionals offering a number of sessions per week to each practice, while others offer one session per month. Thus for example, a CPN and a counsellor might each have weekly sessions at Practice A, and the clinical psychologist and psychiatrist might attend Practice A for sessions on a monthly basis. The number of sessions would be determined by demand, and the duration of each session would be dictated by accepted best practice for the discipline concerned.*

8.1.2   *On Admission to Inpatient Care*

○ Admission is anxiety-provoking for the service user and any accompanying relatives or friends. **Admission staff need to be aware of this at all times and to offer kindly support.**

○ The admission of service users who are in a distressed state is difficult for all concerned, including staff. **Ways and means of dealing with these situations in as non-traumatic a way as possible must be explored**[16].

8.1.3   *On Treatment and Therapy*

○ There is an over-reliance on medication as the only treatment both initially and for the long-term. **Non-pharmacological interventions must become as routine a part of the service as pharmacological treatments now are.** They should include an array of psychological therapies (i.e., art, drama, music and so forth, and not just applied analysis of behaviour, cognitive behaviour therapy, counselling, and psychoanalytic approaches).

○ Communication between service users and their consultants is often unsatisfactory. **The reasons for this need to be explored with consultants and the causes addressed.**

○ People using the publicly funded mental health services cannot choose or change their consultant, therapist or key worker. **Choice of therapist or key worker must be introduced** because – given the nature of mental illness - the relationship of the service user with these professionals is an important element in their therapy and process of recovery.

---

16   Some references to the clinical practice literature on this topic are given in the Bibliography.

8.1.4 *On Inpatient Experience*

O **The organisation of inpatient services is often anti-therapeutic, and over time or where a service user has frequent admissions it promotes de-skilling and institutionalisation.**

O Continuity of care is poor, particularly as associated with the six-monthly rotation of NCHDs. Continuity of care from nursing staff can also be a problem although this is overcome by some facilities who assign 3 nurse key-workers to a service user so that s/he may build a relationship with one person on each nursing roster.

O Facilities offering training in clinical psychology seem to be replicating the organisational flaw that produces the lack of continuity of care arising from the training of psychiatrists. In at least one setting where trainee clinical psychologists deliver therapy programmes the continuity of service users' experience is broken when the trainee is rotated to another placement after some months.

O **In both psychiatry and clinical psychology this flaw can be remedied by planning and overlap between the out-going and in-coming trainees so that when the trainee moves on the individual service user or the group will not experience a major rupture of their care plan.**

O **Service users are often deprived of access to fresh air and exercise**. Some facilities even though built in recent years, do not include a safe outside area like a garden for example, or an indoor exercise area for use in bad weather. This situation seems to have resulted from a lack of reflection on the multi-dimensional nature of mental as opposed to physical illness. Consequently little or no provision was made for the psycho-social as opposed to the medical needs of the user of the mental health service. Features of the lay-out of the facility which are not essential in the acute medical hospital (e.g., the availability of a multi-purpose activity area) pose real problems for the comprehensive care and recovery of persons experiencing mental illness. **These and other problems with the physical environment need immediate attention.** (See also paragraphs **8.3.8 – 8.3.11**)

O The structure of inpatient care follows that of the acute general hospital. **Consultants and nursing staff spend too little time interacting therapeutically with service users.**

O **Night staff** seem to have a purely monitoring function and **appear not to be equipped to take advantages of the therapeutic potential of the fact that night time can be a time when people may be particularly ready to talk, or to be especially in need of support and encouragement.**

○ In general the occupational therapy programme that exist are few; of poor quality; not designed to meet the changing needs of service users as they recover; irregular in their availability; and frequently not delivered by professionally qualified occupational therapists. **The therapeutic and rehabilitative potential of occupational therapy must be realised to its fullest extent by making it a key aspect of the service and having it developed and delivered by qualified occupational therapists.**

○ Service users have little personal privacy, and facilities for entertaining visitors are of a poor standard. Children who visit are not catered for. **New facilities must consider these factors and service providers must consider what changes could be made to existing units.**

○ Seclusion and restraint, or restraint through medication (via a P.R.N note) is fearful for those who experience and those who witness it. **Other options must be explored.**

○ The diverse needs of persons experiencing different kind of mental illness are not accommodated by the structure and organisation of inpatient facilities. **This must be corrected so that the environment is experienced as safe, tranquil and therapeutic.**

8.1.6   *On the Discharge Procedure*

○ Preparation for discharge is not a standard feature of the service and may not even be a routine feature within any given facility. The transition to home would be made easier and the likelihood of relapse would be reduced if the **concerns of service users were addressed before discharge and if they were assured of home visits and/or support telephone contact from CPNs, social workers or personnel in the inpatient unit.**

○ **Carers and families generally must be involved in discharge planning** so that they can offer appropriate support to the service users and can take steps to safeguard themselves against becoming stressed and burnt out.

8.1.7 On Day Care and Ancillary Community Services

○ **Day hospitals are useful only if they offer a well-structured and stimulating range of activities.** The organisational structure of a significant number of day hospitals appear to mirror that of the inpatient facility, including the lack of activities and therapeutic encounters with staff of all kinds.

○ Day centres tend to offer a greater variety of activities and are noted for their more relaxed atmosphere and for the active therapeutic involvement of their staff. **These centres provide a good template for community based mental health care**, although it must be noted that the idea of stigma arising from being seen going to the centres was commented on by a number of research participants.

○ **Services offered by NDTI, FÁS and other similar organisations were singled out for praise and appreciation by service users and carers.** In general the personnel in these organisations appear to work with their clients in ways that are challenging, supportive and encouraging.

○ Short- and long-stay hostels and other forms of 'step down' facilities varying in the levels of support offered to residents are required to aid service users' transition home or to allow them to live safely and comfortable in the community. **This aspect of the public mental health service seems to have been allowed to decline in many locations.**

8.1.8 On Outpatient Services

○ **The organisation of outpatient clinics means that the service is inefficient, and unsatisfactory from the point of view of service users and carers.**

○ The lack of continuity of care is exacerbated beyond that found in the inpatient service because outpatients may not even see their consultant. Rotation of NCHDs continues. The consultants and NCHDs often have no knowledge of the service user's case. Consequently time is wasted and irritation caused to the service user who has to tell his/her story yet again.

○ The type of out-patient contact with an un-familiar consultant or NCHD does not allow for the over-lap solution to the problem of continuity of care suggested for the inpatient setting in paragraph **8.1.4.** However it would improve the experience of service users if the NCHD had prepared for the consultation by **reading service users' notes in advance.**

○ There are indications that a similar problem with continuity of care is emerging in the clinical psychology service. The form of service offered by clinical psychologists does afford the possibility of over-lap between trainees even in outpatients and should be adopted.

○ **Consultation time is too short** for a service user to have any in depth discussion with their clinician should they wish to do so. The remedy for this problem within the current structure of the out patient clinic is not immediately obvious. This matter is raised again in the final point in this paragraph.

○ The practice of booking multiple appointments for the same time affects confidentiality and creates a sense of pressure for the service user who feels s/he must not delay the clinician when others are waiting. **Service providers need to address this problem by considering why the practice of multiple bookings developed, and asking whether the aims of the practice can be achieved in other more client-friendly ways.**

○ **More generally the fact that participants were almost unanimous in their dissatisfaction with the outpatient clinic raises the question of the wisdom of using this structure to deliver service user care in the community.** Service providers, professionals, users and their carers should be consulted to see **whether better use can be made of the resources currently being expended in providing a service which does not perform well in meeting user or carer needs.** It may be that the activities carried out in outpatient clinics at present (monitoring medication; administration of certain types of maintenance medication; renewal of prescriptions) could be provided via a less cumbersome structure, and the resources thus freed used more productively elsewhere in the system.

8.1.9 *On Service User Rights and Advocacy*

○ The apparent absence of rights with regard to accepting or not accepting treatment is a serious concern to service users.

○ The apparent absence of rights of persons admitted involuntarily is also of grave concern.

○ **Service users wondered how well a system of peer advocacy might operate and those with experience of it expressed some concern that this process would not be well received by mental health professionals.**

8.1.10 *On the Experience of Carers*

○ **Carers were generally ignored by the mental health service**. Although their family member more often than not returned to their care or relied on them for support (psychological and material) when not in hospital or at a day hospital or day centre, they were seldom informed of the service users progress or given guidance on how they might help maintain the recovery that had been made.

○ Their own health needs, which would naturally arise in the stressful circumstance in which they live, were never addressed. Carers noted instances of being left waiting without support during the admission of a family member, and service users themselves mentioned that their families were not given the support they needed to cope with their (service users') admission, treatment, or rehabilitation.

○ Carers' insights into the needs of their family member were rarely sought, and when volunteered were generally not welcomed by mental health professionals.

○ It is past the time when carers should be seen as partners with service users, mental health professionals, and service planners and providers in creating a quality mental health service. **Their views must be actively sought and their insights acted upon. Reasons must be given for not acting on carers' suggestions. All communication must be clear and ambiguity of language and defensive attitudes must be avoided. Their need for psychological support must be responded to.**

8.2.0 Observations

8.2.1 Before moving on to look at the practical significance of these findings we note that their similarity to those of other studies in Ireland (Elliot & Mason, 2000; Brosnan, Collins, Dempsey et al., 2002; Sainsbury Centre for Mental Health, 2003; Southern Health Board (undated); Quality in Mental Health - your views, MHC 2005) and elsewhere (Acuff, 2000; Camden Mental Health Consortium, 2005; Quirk & Lelliott,2001; Wood & Pistrang, 2004) indicates the validity of the results of this project. As indicated in the Technical Note (Appendix V), the process of establishing validity through 'triangulation' involves showing the presence of similar trends and themes when data is collected in different ways.

SECTION EIGHT

8.2.2 Turning to the service-quality aspect, few of the views and experiences of the service users and carers who took part in this enquiry will come as a surprise to mental health professionals, to mental health service managers and their employers, or to the members of the Mental Health Commission. What is more surprising about these findings is that they reiterate a position that continues to exist, although a substantial body of research on effective clinical and nursing practice, and models of service delivery in mental health care has been available for a considerable number of years. Although the literature on practice elsewhere shows that the Irish state mental health service is not unique in experiencing the problems described, this does not explain the failure of Irish services to ensure that their service is exemplary. Keogh (2005) discusses the role of a well-planned national programme of mental health research in ensuring the development and delivery of an effective service, and the absence of such a programme in Ireland probably does contribute to the under or uneven development of services here. However, for reasons given next, this cannot be the full explanation.

8.2.3 A quite cursory search of databases on the relevant applied research literature in medicine, nursing, clinical psychology and health service management yielded the articles listed in the Bibliography at the end of this report. This literature addresses problems with the mental health service raised by the participants in this study. For example, empirical studies of the impact on such variables as treatment compliance and recovery of communication between the consultant and service user are reviewed by Cruz & Pincus, (2002). The issue of seclusion and restraint has been studied by Brown & Tooke, (1992); Breeze & Repper, (1998); Donat (1998); Earle Williams & Myers,(2001); Kaltiala-Henio, Tuohimaki, Korkelia, & Lehtinen, (2003) and viable alternatives have been proposed. The problem of over-medication through the use of unmonitored P.R.N (as needed) notes has been researched by Thapa, Palmer, Owen et al., (2003), who show how the problem can be avoided. Research by Corley and Goren (1998) and Lauber, Ajdacid-Grosse, and Roessler (2004) on the stigmatised view that some professionals can have of a client group casts some light on the negative and non-therapeutic behaviour of a minority of such professionals towards those in their care.

8.2.4 Further, the admittedly few but none the less noted instances of user satisfaction across all disciplines raises the question '**Why is this level of service satisfaction not the norm?'**

8.2.5 Four inter-related factors are put forward for consideration in attempting to answer this question. They are:

- **Organisation of the service**

- **Custom and practice developed within each catchment area or treatment facility over time**

- **Professional education**

- **Variables related to the individual professional**

8.2.6 **Organisation of the publicly funded mental health service** is based on the model of the acute general medical hospital. We suggest here and argue further below (paragraphs **8.3.4, 8.3.8 - 8.3.9**) that because physical and mental illness differ from each other in such fundamental ways, the organisational structures for physical health care delivery cannot work for the mental health care services. The following examples illustrate the point.

The pattern of interaction of mental health professionals with inpatients is dictated by the acute medical illness model and as we have seen from the data presented in this report, lack of continuity of care by NHCDs and trainee clinical psychologists, and disrupted contact with nursing staff due to rostering arrangements reduces the therapeutic potential of inpatient care to a critical degree.

Outpatient services based on the physical illness model assume that appointments require a short period of time with little need for in-depth discussion about the service user's current life situation. Community services are resourced only to the extent of being able to provide a crisis service, and this too reflects the relative underdevelopment of this aspect of care in the primary health care service and in the public health nursing service. Since persons with physical illness return to home and work quite quickly, and senior citizens who require nursing home care may do so only for a short time, the concept of supported accommodation for the intermediate or long term is new and generally not well planned or resourced.

Duration as an inpatient is expected to be a matter of weeks at the most so that boredom and a need for opportunities for outdoor or indoor physical exercise are unlikely to arise. However the now widely recognised risk to physical health created by physical inactivity may be particularly acute for users of the mental health service, many of whom are concerned about the weight gain associated with their medication. This tendency to gain weight is exacerbated by the lack of amenities for physical activity and the fact that inpatient facilities and day hospitals tend to promote a sedentary life style, (see extracts in 'Daily Life in the Inpatient Facility' in Sections 4 and 5.

8.2.7 Like any organisation, **each inpatient facility will establish its own forms of custom and practice** over time. Admission procedures for disturbed service users; when and how seclusion and/or restraint take place; and the administration of medication (use of P.R.N orders for example) will differ between facilities. There will sometimes be within-facility variation depending upon the views and preferences of individual members of staff. Some of the available literature on the issues just listed was mentioned in paragraph **8.2.3**. In the light of available knowledge, it is reasonable to ask that established custom and practice should be reviewed and other methods that would be less traumatic for service users and for staff be adopted. The points on communication and engagement raised later in paragraph **8.2.10** will also apply in the inpatient setting.

8.2.8 Theoretical knowledge and evidence-based practice is part of the 'stock in trade' of the **professional training** offered by medical and nursing schools, and the various medical, nursing, psychological, social work and other professional bodies. The medical and nursing schools offer courses at undergraduate, postgraduate and post-experience levels. As well as representing the interests of their members, many of the professional bodies design, oversee, assess and register professionals in their speciality disciplines. They also concern themselves with issues of continuous professional development (CPD). The scientific validity of the professional education and training received by practitioners of the various disciplines relevant to mental health is not relevant to this research project. However it is appropriate to point out that service users find certain aspects of their treating professionals' understanding of, approach to, and treatment of their mental illness unsatisfactory. This is particularly so with regard to the dominance of the organic approach to mental ill health and the consequent reliance on polypharmacy and long-term medication in its treatment. The research evidence on the nature of mental illness shows that it involves a complexity of factors. Physiological vulnerability, psychological vulnerability and triggering events all play a part. The relative contribution of each factor is variable across conditions and between persons. The roles of psychological and social factors in creating the conditions for the emergence and maintenance of various psychological states appear to need more emphasis than they currently receive in professional undergraduate and specialist training[17].

8.2.9 When service users report satisfactory contact with professionals, this is usually because the latter engage with them as unique persons. This aspect of the service is under the control of the **individual professional** to a very great extent. Thus in the clinical consultation for example, each clinician is free to decide whether or not to invite the service user to tell his/her story, to discuss it and the person's current

---

17   One might even debate whether the education of mental health professionals should become a specialist stream at an early stage in the undergraduate curriculum so that it is made a clear vocational choice and there is sufficient time available for in-depth training in the complexities of the relevant aspects of the medical, psychological and social sciences.

situation, and to explain treatment options and their likely outcomes. While the detail of what the contact with practitioners from different disciplines involves will differ, the issue of whether there is open communication and interested engagement with the service user is the same. In so far as the individual professional has control in this way, personal motivation and interest in the job, and habits acquired through formal education and the observation of peers at work are where we must look to make changes in the interpersonal aspect of the quality of the service user's experience.

8.2.10 It will probably have struck the reader that these four factors do not function in isolation from each other. Thus for example, the mismatch between the model of service delivery with the nature of mental disorder can create problems for the individual professional. Even the most highly motivated consultant psychiatrist cannot engage in detailed discussion with a service user when the time allowed for outpatient consultations is short, and both practitioner and service user know that others are waiting. As mentioned earlier, the roster system for nursing care in the inpatient setting is again a reflection of work practices that are suited to the care of physically ill persons. As experienced by service users, it leads to discontinuity of contact with them[18], and seems to define the nurse's role in terms of the administration of drugs, bed making, and symptom-focused note keeping. The emergence of the lack of continuity of care in the psychological aspect of the mental health service in some locations shows how an unsuitable model of service delivery can reproduce the deficiencies of one area of a service (the rotation of non-consultant medics) in another (the training of clinical psychologists)[19].

8.3.0 Suggested Strategic Actions

8.3.1 It would be advisable that the starting point in responding to the views of service users as expressed here (and in other reports) be one where there is a realistic chance of success. It would also be important that the concerns of professionals affected by any changes and their education/training needs in any new dispensation are fully acknowledged and met in practical ways.

8.3.2 Building on the issues discussed in Part II of this report under the heading 'Towards Changing Practice', the important area of communication with service users would be one starting point with a reasonable chance of success in the short to intermediate term. It is assumed that the Mental Health Commission will fulfil its mission to 'foster and promote high standards of delivery of mental health services' by identifying, advocating, and actively supporting all practical initiatives that can achieve this.

---

18   *One facility solved this problem by assigning a service user one key-worker on each shift (see p.56 and 8.1.4.)*

19   *See suggested solution in 8.1.4.*

Accordingly the Commission might consider producing a briefing paper on 'communication and engagement with service users' in which the therapeutic advantages and job satisfaction of professionals are outlined and supporting research evidence cited. This document could become the focus of workshops run on the Commission's behalf (or simply with its encouragement, or in conjunction with the DOHC's Expert Group) in which professionals discuss among themselves and with representatives of service users why communication and engagement is not uniformly very good. Changing one's attitude to and style of interacting with others does not require financial resources. Positioning professionals to meet the psychological costs arising from increased engagement with the service user can be done through ongoing professional development in the immediate term, and should be made a key part of undergraduate and postgraduate professional training.

8.3.3 The issue of professionals' communication and liaison with carers and carers' roles in the lives of service users could be approached in a similar fashion. Service providers and their professional staff cannot continue to ignore the contribution being made by this important group. Support from the Commission in presenting their case for information, some training in strategies that they could use to diffuse or cope with difficult situations with their family member, and some personal support, would help to sustain this valuable element within community based care.

8.3.4 Working through its Inspectorate of Mental Health Services the Commission could open discussions with the clinical managers of the various inpatient facilities throughout the country on alternative ways for dealing with critical incidents in patient care, and on controlling the risk of over-medication, (of course other topics can also be addressed). Interested facilities might be asked to engage in pilot studies of new modes of intervention based upon the findings in the research literature. Again there does not seem to be any need for direct financial investment in such a change. Care has to be given in any event, and systematically exploring psychological and behavioural options which may improve users' care and develop the skills of the professionals involved is not fundamentally different from introducing a new medical intervention. Demonstrating that alternative approaches work will provide a convincing argument for their general use throughout the service, and the pilot sites could act as centres of excellence for training in these methods. (Even well-established interventions can need modification depending on circumstances, so the pilot site professionals will acquire and pass on particular knowledge which will go beyond that available in the published literature).

8.3.5 Liaising with the education and training schools in the third level institutions and with the professional bodies concerned with training, registration, and continuing professional development will be necessary to ensure that they are all aware of the Commission's concern that graduates and specialists in the disciplines relevant to mental health are in a position to offer services of the highest quality. This process may be facilitated within third level institutions at least by the emergence of quality assurance initiatives. Again financial resources do not appear to be a major requirement for action in this area.

8.3.6   The organisational structure of the publicly funded adult mental health service is based on the acute general hospital model and is unsuited to the needs of persons experiencing mental illness. Although health system reform is ongoing at present, there seems to be little debate about the position of the mental health services within any new arrangement or of service delivery models suited to the Irish situation. For example, the various innovative community based models should be examined to see how they might apply in other catchments. It may be timely for the Commission to highlight to planners the importance of looking at the *particularity* of mental health care rather than continuing to see it as a version of physical medicine.

8.3.7   Significant financial investment is implied in the need for multi-disciplinary inputs to service user care at primary, inpatient and community care levels. At present these teams are not always fully staffed, and the commitment to some elements (e.g. occupational therapy; various forms of psychotherapy; counselling; community social work) seems less than serious. In this context the under funding of the mental health service, and the trend towards cutting the overall amount allocated and spreading what remains too thinly, or reactively withdrawing funding from one aspect of the service to provide for the needs of another when service user and/or carer pressure is brought to bear, must be of critical concern to the Commission. Any argument that the Commission might wish to make for the necessity to provide adequate levels of staff can be supported by reference to the research literature on the therapeutic needs of adult users of the mental health services. Research from health economics would also help to make the case for real and sustained investment in mental health.

8.3.8   There is a real need to think more creatively and therapeutically about the physical design and décor of inpatient facilities, day hospitals and day centres. Shared sleeping accommodation and the lack of personal privacy are obvious areas for action. The absence of a multi-purpose activity area, and safe access to the outdoors in some facilities is not only critical for reasons related to general physical health: it can also affect the person's psychological state. Thus a sense of apathy and despondency can be created by confinement indoors and the sedentary life-style it may promote. The emotional pressure created by the constant presence of others and by a noisy or busy environment would be alleviated by opportunities to walk outside or to use a gym or similar area.

8.3.9 The physical environment also needs to be made more 'controllable' by offering service users a variety of spaces other than the dormitory or day room, and the apparently constant exposure to TV that is a feature of the latter. Small, comfortable sitting rooms where a service user might talk privately with a staff member; go when in need of quietness, or to read, chat, play board games or cards with others; or use to entertain their visitors will enhance the therapeutic impact of the in-patient or day hospital setting. These kinds of changes will also require significant investment but would significantly improve service user experience[20]. They would be cost effective over time if measures such as reduced instances of disruptive behaviour, and reduced staff stress (and absenteeism), and improved levels and speed of recovery were included in the reckoning.

8.3.10 The Commission can have a valuable role in requiring redress of the deficiencies in the physical environment of existing facilities in so far as is possible, and insisting that it have oversight of the plans and construction of all facilities in the future.

20   *It may be possible to deploy existing space in ways which would go some way towards implementing changes at moderate cost.*

SECTION EIGHT

After Word

Viewed as a totality the changes required to achieve a quality state mental health service for adult service users are daunting. However they do not have to be tackled as a single mammoth task that must be accomplished 'in one fell swoop' as it were. The various initiatives taking place within different former health boards (now Health Service Executive) or within individual facilities, are evidence of the desire of providers and staff to develop a service that is therapeutic for the user and that staff themselves are satisfied with and proud to be part of. They also provide the foundations on which the kinds of developments identified as necessary by the participants in this survey can be built.

Ongoing and 'planned-but-not-yet-implemented' efforts need to be collated so that the Commission has a clear view of what is happening at present. It may be appropriate for it to actively encourage these local or regional initiatives irrespective of their stage of development by offering suggestions based on the expertise within its own ranks, or by putting providers and professionals in touch with appropriate outside resources. The activities suggested in the paragraphs following **8.3.0** can be introduced in a rolling programme of action research designed to achieve the overall goal of a quality service through incremental change. What is most important at this juncture is that stakeholders, with particular focus on service users and carers, can soon begin to see and experience significant albeit small changes in the service rather than that their hopes should be raised through unrealistic promises that are neither sustained or sustainable.

A key aspect of the presence of the Mental Health Commission within the health system is its position as the rallying point for those with a stake in mental health in Ireland. As such it can unify existing and planned initiatives with the aspirations of providers, professionals, service users, and carers into a coherent programme for service development. Given its statutory remit, it can be the stakeholders' voice powerfully articulating the case, backed up by this and other research, for realistic, sustained, and ring-fenced investment in mental health.

Bibliography

Items marked with an asterix (*) refer to publications mentioned in the report. The other items included may be relevant to readers with particular interests.

*Acuff, C. (2000). Commentary: Listening to the Message. *Journal of Clinical Psychology, Vol.* **56**; 11: 1459-1465.

Benson, A., Secker, J., Balfe, E., Lipsedge, M., Robinson, S. & Walker, J. (2003). Discourses of blame: accounting for aggression and violence on an acute mental health inpatient unit. *Social Science & Medicine;* **57**: 917-926.

Berland, A. (2001). Mental Health Reform in British Columbia: toward innovation, equity and accountability. *Administration and Policy in Mental Health;* **29(1)**: 1-10.

*Breeze, J.A. & Repper, J. (1998). Struggling for control: the care experiences of 'difficult' patients in mental health services. *Journal of Advanced Nursing;* **28(6)**; 1301-1311.

*Brosnan, E., Collins, S., Dempsey, H., Dermody, F., Maguire, L., Maria, Morris, N. (2002) *Pathways Report: Experiences of Mental Health Services from a User-led Perspective.* Western Health Board.

*Brown, J.S. & Tooke, S.K. (1992). On the Seclusion of Psychiatric Patients. *Social Sciences in Medicine;* **35(5)**; 711-721.

*Camden Mental Health Consortium: www.cmhc.org.uk

Carr Communications (2004) *Speaking Your Mind: Summary of Submissions to the Expert Group on Mental health.* Dublin: Department of Health and Children. Viewable and downloadable from the Expert Group's website www.mentalhealthpolicy.ie

Carrick, R., Mitchell, A., Powell, R.A. & Lloyd, K. (2004). The quest for wellbeing: a qualitative study of the experience of taking antipsychotic medication. *Psychology and Psychotherapy.* **77(1)**: 19-33.

Christensen, A. & Jacobson, N.S. (1994). Who (Or What) Can Do Psychotherapy: the status and challenge of non-professional therapies. *Psychological Science.* **5(1)**: 8-14.

*Corley, M.C. & Goren, S. (1998). The Dark Side of Nursing: Impact of Stigmatising Responses on Patients. *Scholarly Inquiry for Nursing Practice: An International Journal,* **12 (2)**.

*Crawford, M.J., & Rutter, D. (2004). Are the views of members of mental health user groups representative of those of 'ordinary' patients? A cross-sectional survey of service users and providers. *Journal of Mental Health,* **13 (6)**: 561-568.

Crowe, K. (2004) *What We Heard.* Report of a survey by Irish Advocacy Network for the Expert Group on Mental Health Policy. Dublin: Department of Health and Children.

Viewable and downloadable from the Expert Group's site www.mentalhealthpolicy.ie

*Cruz, M. & Pincus, H.A. (2002). Research on the Influence that Communication in Psychiatric Encounters has on Treatment. *Psychiatric Services;* **53**: 1253-1265.

Davidson, L., Chinman, M., Kloos, B., Weingarten, R., Stayner, D. & Kraemer Tebes, J. (1999). Peer Support Among Individuals With Severe Mental Illness: A review of the evidence. *Clinical Psychology: Science and Practice.* *6(2)*: 165-187.

Department of Health and Children Mental Health Act 2001 stationery office, Dublin.

*Donat, D.C. (1998). Impact of a mandatory behavioural consultation on seclusion/restraint utilization in a psychiatric hospital. *Journal of Behaviour Therapy and Experimental Psychiatry;* *29*: 13-19.

Dunne, E.A. & Fitzpatrick, A.C. (1999). The views of professionals on the role of self-help groups in the mental health area. *Irish Journal of Psychiatric Medicine;* *16(3)*: 84-89.

*Earle Williams, J. & Myers, R.E. (2001). Relationship of less restrictive interventions with seclusion/restraints usage, average years of psychiatric experience, and staff mix. *Journal of the American Psychiatric Nurses Association;* *7(5)*: 139-144.

*Elliott, I. & Mason, T. (2000). *Unique Insight: a report on the consultation with users of the St. Loman's Mental Health Service*. South Western Area Health Board.

Fitzpatrick, L., Dunne, E.A., O'Sullivan, M., & Cole, M (1995) *Alternative Acute Care: A Study in Mental Health Care*. Catherine St., Limerick: Mid-Western Health Board.

Gastmans, C. (1999). Care As A Moral Attitude in Nursing. *Nursing Ethics;* *6(3)*: 214-223.

Hartrick Doane, G.A. (2002). Am I Still Ethical? The socially-mediated process of nurses' moral identity. *Nursing Ethics;* *9(6)*: 623-635.

*Hickey, T., Moran, R., & Walsh, D. (2003) *Psychiatric Day Care- An Underused Option?* Dublin: Health Research Board.

Humphreys, K., Phibbs, C.S. & Moos, R.H. (1996). Addressing Self-Selection Effects in Evaluations of Mutual Help Groups and Professional Mental Health Services: an introduction to two-stage sample selection models. *Evaluation and Program Planning;* *19(4)*: 301-308.

Humphreys, K., & Rappaport, J. (1994). Researching self-help/mutual aid groups and organisations: many roads, one journey. *Applied & Preventive Psychology;* *3*: 217-231.

*Kaltiala-Heino, R., Tuohimaki, C., Korkeila, J. & Lehtinen, V. (2003). Reasons for Using Seclusion and Restraint in Psychiatric Inpatient Care. *International Journal of Law and Psychiatry, 26*, 139-149.

*Keogh, F. (2005). *Research Strategy*. Dublin. Mental Health Commission 2005.

*Know Your Audience: Ch. 2 (Part A); downloaded from www.audiencedialogue.org on 06/01/05.

*Lauber, C., Anthony, M., Ajdacic-Gross, V., Roessler, W. (2004). What about psychiatrists' attitude to mentally ill people? *European Psychiatry.* *19(7):* 423-7.

Link, B.G. & Phelan, J.C. (2001). Conceptualising Stigma. *Annual Review of Sociology.* **27**: 363-385.

Mid-Western Health Board (1998). *Mental Health Strategy*. Catherine Street, Limerick.

Montgomery, P. (2001). Shifting Meaning of Asylum. *Journal of Advanced Nursing*. **33(4)**: 425-31.

Nairn, R., Coverdale, J. & Claasen, D. (2001). From source material to news story in New Zealand print media: a prospective study of the stigmatising processes in depicting mental illness. *Australian and New Zealand Journal of Psychiatry.* **35**: 654-659.

Niveau, G. (2004). Preventing human rights abuses in psychiatric establishments: the work of the CPT. European Psychiatry. www.elsevier.com/locate/eurpsy

Quality in Mental Health – Your Views. Dublin: Mental Health Commission 2005.

*Quirk, A. & Lelliott, P. (2001). What do we know about life on acute psychiatric wards in the UK? A review of the research evidence. *Social Science & Medicine;* **53**: 1565-1574.

Ralph, R.O., Lambert, D., & Kidder, K.A. *The Recovery Perspective and Evidence-Based Practice for People with Serious Mental Illness.* Working paper from Behavioural Health Recovery Management Project developed by the authors at Edmund S. Muskie School of Public Service, University of South Maine, U.S.A.

Ruggeri, M. & Tansella, M. (2002). To what extent do mental health services meet patients' needs and provide satisfactory care? *Current Opinion in Psychiatry.* **15**: 193-199.

Rush, B. (2004). Mental health service user involvement in England: lessons from history. *Journal of Psychiatric and mental health nursing.* **11(3)**: 313-8.

Rutter, D., Manley, C., Weaver, T., Crawford, M.J. & Fulop, N. (2003). Patients or partners? Case studies of user involvement in the planning and delivery of adult mental health services in London. Social Science & Medicine. www.elsevier.com/locate/socscimed

*Sainsbury Centre for Mental Health (2003). *A New Service Model for Mental Health Services in the North-Western Region.* Letterkenny. North-Western Health Board.

Salem, D.A. Reischl, T.M., Gallacher, F. & Weaver Randall, K. (2000). The Role of Referent and Expert Power in Mutual Help. *American Journal of Community Psychology;* **28(3)**: 303-324.

Schizophrenia Ireland/Lucia Foundation and the Irish Psychiatric Association (2003). *Towards Recovery: Principles of good practice in the treatment, care, rehabilitation and recovery of people with a diagnosis of schizophrenia and related mental disorders*.

Simpson, E.L. & House, A.O. (2003). User and care involvement in mental health services: from rhetoric to science. *British Journal of Psychiatry;* **183**: 89-91.

Soloff, P.H. (1978). Behavioural Precipitants of Restraint in the Modern Milieu. *Comprehensive Psychiatry;* **19(2)**: 179-184.

Southern Health Board. *Focussing Minds...Developing Mental Health Services in Cork and Kerry*. (Report not dated).

*Thapa, P.B., Palmer, S.L., Owen, R.R., Huntley, A.L., Clardy, J.A. & Miller, L.H. (2003). P.R.N. (As-Needed) Orders and Exposure of Psychiatric Inpatients to Unnecessary Psychotropic Medications. *Psychiatric Services;* **54**: 1282-1286.

Thornicroft, G., Tansella, M., Becker, T., Knapp, M., Leese, M., Schene, A. & Vazquez-Barquero, J.L. (2003). The personal impact of schizophrenia in Europe. Schizophrenia Research. www.elsevier.com/locate/schres

The Irish College of Psychiatrists (2003). *Psychiatry Training in the Republic of Ireland: A resource book for trainees*.

Van Ommeren, M., Saxena, S., Loretti, A., Saraceno, B. (2003). Ensuring care for patients in custodial psychiatric hospitals in emergencies. *The Lancet;* **362**: 574.

*Western Health Board / Schizophrenia Ireland (2002). *Pathways Report: Experiences of Mental Health Services from a User-Led Perspective*.

Williams, J. & Lindley, P. (1996). Working with Mental Health Service Users to Change Mental Health Services. *Journal of Community & Applied Social Psychology:* **6**, 1-14.

*Wilson, C., Narin, R., Coverdale, J., & Panapa, A. (1999). Constructing mental illness as dangerous: a pilot study. *Australian and New Zealand Journal of Psychiatry:* **33**; 240-247.

*Wood, D. & Pistrang, N. (2004). A Safe Place? Service Users' Experiences of an Acute Mental Health ward. *Journal of Community & Applied Social Psychology: **14:** 16-28.

Appendices

Appendix I

Information Supplied to Potential Participants

INFORMATION FOR PARTICIPANTS IN SERVICE USERS' SURVEY (FOCUS GROUP SECTION)

1. The focus group session will be for 24 hours. There will be 2 hours of discussion and a 15 minute break for refreshment.

2. There will be 2 people involved in running the group.

3. You are guaranteed total anonymity for any views you express. This means that while we would like to be able to use your words to make a point in our report on the usefulness of services to users, **we will not in any way attribute it to the person who says those words.**

4. **Our reason for using the words of participants** (but not attributing it to any person) is because how people who have first hand experience talk about something often has much more impact than someone making the point on their behalf.

5. **We would like you to give us permission to tape the session, so as to make sure that we get the views expressed as accurate as possible.** If you allow us to do this, the tape will be listened to only by the researchers. It will be kept in the strong room of our Department for 1 year after the report has been submitted to the Mental Health Commission and it will then be destroyed.

6. The areas to be covered in our discussion with you are:

   i) Initial consultation – experience with

      GP/ Consultant/ Psychologist/Social Worker/Other

   ii) Psychiatric Treatment – experience of

      Medication / ECT / Other

   iii) In Patient Service – experience of

      Nursing care / Care attendants / Other patients / Occupational therapy Group therapy / Individual psychological therapy
      Living environment (including feeling safe/opportunities for privacy/physical layout/access to local community/possibility for activities and entertainment not related to therapy).

iv) Day Hospital Service – experience of

**Nursing care / Occupational therapy / Social workers' services
Individual psychological therapy / Group therapy / Psychiatric treatment
Psychiatric consultation / Psychological consultation / Rehabilitation
service**

v) Out Patient Service – experience of

**Community nursing support/care / Rehabilitation service / Contact with
mutual help groups / Clinic visits**

vi) Treatment Plan

Is there one? – ('Can you tell me about it – what it involves?')

What was your input to it?

Is it reviewed? ('Is it discussed with you – how its working for you…..?)

We will send a summary of our conclusions for your group to each participant (via your
organisation to ensure your anonymity) and you will have an opportunity to correct anything
we might have misunderstood. We will include those amendments in our report to the
Commission.

Dr. Elizabeth Dunne, (Principal Investigator)

Department of Applied Psychology, University College, Cork.

Letter of Invitation and Information on the Project (Independents Section)

My name is Elizabeth Dunne and I am a lecturer and researcher in the Department of Applied Psychology in University College, Cork.

Our Department has been contracted by the Mental Health Commission to interview users of the mental health services such as yourself in order to get your views on the services you have used. We would like to hear from you about the services you found most helpful and to find out what changes you think should be made to improve the services for yourself and others in the future.

If you would be willing to talk to us, we guarantee that your views will be kept totally confidential and your name will not be mentioned in our report to the Commission or anywhere else. The views you express will not be passed on to anybody else in the health service either. What we want to do is to pool the experiences and opinions of a large number of service users so we can get a general view of the developments in the service they would find useful.

I would like to assure you that participation is totally voluntary and that your present or future care will not be affected by whether you decide to take part or not.

Each interview will take about 30 – 40 minutes. It will involve just one interviewer and yourself and it will take place in a private room. A list of the areas we would like to talk with you about is attached to this page. I would also like to stress that if you should wish to take a break or to end the interview at any point, you will be totally free to do so.

We would like to be able to tape record the interview with you so we can be sure that we have an accurate picture of your views. However, if you would prefer not to have the interview taped, we will be happy to just make notes of what you have to say.

I hope you will decide to take part in the project, but at all events thank you very much for considering this request. If you would like to contact me to discuss the possibility of taking part in more detail, please feel free to 'phone me at 021- 4904505 or write to me at the Department of Applied Psychology, University College, Cork.

With best wishes,

Yours sincerely,

Dr. **Elizabeth Dunne**, Ph.D

Topics to be discussed with you

Initial consultation – your experience with:

GP/ Consultant/ Psychologist/Social Worker/Other

Psychiatric Treatment /Psychological Therapies/Social Work Interventions – your experience of:

Medication

ECT

Cognitive behaviour therapy etc.

In Patient Service – your experience of:

Nursing care

Care attendants

Other patients

Occupational therapy

Group therapy

Individual psychological therapy

Living environment (including feeling safe/opportunities for privacy/physical layout/access to local community/possibility for activities and entertainment not related to therapy).

Day Hospital Service – your experience of:

Nursing care

Occupational therapy

Social workers' services

Individual psychological therapy

Group therapy

Psychiatric treatment

Psychiatric consultation

Psychological consultation

Rehabilitation service

Out Patient Service – your experience of:

Community nursing support/care

Rehabilitation service

Contact with mutual help groups

Clinic visits

Treatment Plan – the programme of medication and other therapies set out to treat your problems and assist your recovery.

Appendix II

Consent by Service User for Participation in Research Protocol

Protocol Number:

Identification Number for this Study:

Title of Protocol:

Doctor(s) Directing Research: Dr. Elizabeth Dunne

1.   I confirm that I have received a copy of the Information Sheet for the above study. I have read it and I understand it. I have received an explanation of the nature, purpose, duration of the study and what my involvement will be.

2.   I have had time to consider whether to take part in this study and I have had the opportunity to ask questions.

3.*   I give permission for my interview with the researcher to be taped

or

4.   I give permission for a written record to be made of my interview with the researcher.

5.   I give permission for my words to be used in the report written by the researcher on the clear understanding that those words will not be attributed to me personally.

6.   I understand that my participation is voluntary and that I am free to withdraw at any time, without giving any reason, without my medical care or legal rights being affected.

7.   I understand that my consultant, Dr ..... , will be informed by Dr. Dunne that I am taking part in this study.

8.   I understand that sections of any of my medical notes may be looked at by responsible individuals from _____ Hospital. I understand that it will not be necessary for the researchers to view my file. I give permission for the relevant persons from the hospital to have access to my records for the purposes of this study.

9.   I agree to take part in the above study.

_____   _____   _____

Name of patient   Date   Signature

_____   _____   _____

Name of person taking consent   Date   Signature

(*if different from investigator*)

_____   _____   _____

Investigator   Date   Signature

1 copy for patient, 1 copy for investigator, 1 copy for medical records

3* Please put a line through the option that you do not want to follow.

Appendix III

General Points on approach for Focus Groups and for Individual Interviews

The purpose of the study is to get an understanding of the **experience** of the people who use the mental health services. Broadly speaking we want to find out how users experienced accessing the mental health services initially and subsequently.

For example :

* Was referral discussed with them – were different options explained and were they given a say in which to use?

* Do they feel 'sent' or do they 'go' to clinics etc?

* What has their experience of treatment/therapy been like (were options discussed? possible side-effects explained?)

* Was there a regular review of progress and discussion of their experience of the treatment/therapy and how it was affecting their lives?

* Was the service delivered in a friendly, caring way, and personally respectful way?

* Did they feel safe and at ease in the treatment setting (in day hospital; clinic; residential unit etc.)

While we must cover the topic areas, the probes can be flexible. Please feel free to substitute your own or come up with new ones as your discussion with each group unfolds.

PLEASE USE OPEN QUESTIONS SO THAT PARTICIPANTS ARE NOT 'LED' IN ANY WAY. For example, with the enquiry about referral use the format

'Can you tell me about the first time you saw a professional person about the problems you were having? ....who was that person? ....and what did (GP) say?

Other examples –

'What did that (treatment) consist of?

'What kinds of things did you do there (at the Day Centre)

' How did that (treatment/contact) help you?

'What would you suggest the service does about that situation based on your experience of it?

Discission guide for focus groups and Individual Interviews

Initial consultation –

GP/ Consultant/ Psychologist/Social Worker/Other

Psychiatric Treatment /Psychological Therapies/Social Work Interventions –

Medication (including choice of drug/side-effects,etc.)

ECT

Cognitive behaviour therapy etc.

In Patient Service –

Nursing care

Care attendants

Other patients

Occupational therapy

Group therapy

Individual psychological therapy

Living environment (including feeling safe/opportunities for privacy/physical layout/access to local community/possibility for activities and entertainment not related to therapy).

Day Hospital Service –

Nursing care

Occupational therapy

Social workers' services

Individual psychological therapy

Group therapy

Psychiatric treatment

Psychiatric consultation

Psychological consultation

Rehabilitation service (including career guidance/training/ education/ social skills development.

Out Patient Service –

Community nursing support/care

Rehabilitation service

Contact with mutual help groups

Clinic visits (including ease of consultation with all members of mental health team).

Treatment Plan – the programme of medication and other therapies set out treat the person's problem and assist their recovery.

Mental Health Commission project on views of the users of the publically funded mental health services

GUIDELINES FOR THE FOCUS GROUPS

1. The focus group session will be for 2¼ hours approximately. There will be 2 hours of discussion and a 15 minute break for refreshment. Please allow 10 minutes or so for 'winding down' and please be alert to anybody appearing to be extra tired etc. at the end of the session. If you think that someone is so, have a quiet word with them to ensure they have someone to go home with or someone at home. A contact for each group has been organised to give support to anyone in the group who might need it. We can also expect that given the nature of the groups, people will be fairly caring of each other.

2. The moderator will introduce the questions and the co-moderator will write points raised by the participants on a flip chart. This is just to keep things focused and to help people home in on what is being said. Either moderator might ask about something that strikes them, but generally please allow the discussion to be led by the participants themselves. If people are going off the track; taking over the group; telling long stories etc. please gently re-focus them! The suggested Introductory Remarks that you will have to hand should help prevent this, or should prepare the ground for an intervention if that is necessary.

3. Reiterate at the start that total anonymity for any views expressed is guaranteed, and reassure people on this briefly at the end. There is no need to go into a long spiel on it. Just mention it and move on. Again, we expect to have cleared the issue of taping in advance, but if it should arise and looks like taking a lot of time to resolve, just move on to taking notes. This means the co-moderator will be a busy person! So the moderator should take over writing on the flip chart with the co-moderators doing their best to get the context for the comments. Working from the charts and from the co-moderators' notes we should be able to make sense of the views expressed.

4. Towards the end of the meeting (say about 20 minutes from scheduled end) the co-moderator should list the 6 top concerns of the group.

5. Please tell the group that we will send a summary of our understanding of the issues they raised to each member (via their organisation to ensure their anonymity) and each person will have an opportunity to correct anything we might have misunderstood. We will include those amendments in our report to the Commission.

GUIDE LINES FOR INTERVIEWERS

1. Introduce yourself - "Hello Mr./ Ms/ Mrs. X. I'm Mary Murphy. Would you like to sit here etc.

2. "Would you mind if I called you by your first name? (If the participant is a senior, don't ask this and continue to address them as Mr./Ms/Mrs. unless **they** very specifically tell you to use their first name).

3. It is best to dress middle-of-the-road style. Too casual clothes can seem disrespectful and unprofessional and too smart can be as bit overwhelming and inhibiting to some people.

4. Please be aware that some people may have allergies to the chemicals involved in perfume or to certain aromas, so go easy on the perfume and on the after shave!

5. If you need to make notes, tell the person what you are doing and why. Please don't just start in without some explanation as - apart from the politeness factor – this can be intimidating and makes the person feel like a specimen.

6. **NEVER** volunteer a view on the issue under discussion, or give your own opinion, or give advice. That is not the researcher's business at all. If someone raises an issue of concern, identify with them one of their team to whom they can talk. Say something like, "I wouldn't be able to give you any idea/help/opinion on that. But would you talk to your XXXX? or to YYYY? about it? If the person seems stuck on the issue, say, "It would be a good idea to talk to your XXX about that matter. Now lets look at...." and move them gently on to the next topic.

7. **If you have a concern about a participant's welfare after the interview, notify the senior nurse or other responsible staff member. Keep it factual! Please also notify the person we liaise with on the Board, and the study director.** I will be raising this issue at the meeting with the Health Boards prior to the start of the Independents' interviews so we should have a clear procedure to follow.

8. Remember **all views expressed are totally confidential**. If anyone in the hospital/hostel/clinic/workshop/day centre asks you about the results, please just say general things like " Very good – very interesting – people are very helpful." Also please **do not** make the project the focus of a conversation with friends. You may say more than you meant to or people might pick you up incorrectly. **You will be affected by people's stories and experiences.** But please can we keep discussion of that for our meetings as a team.

Appendix IV

Summary of four group findings for each focus groups

Mental Health Commission Study

Focus Group #1

Dear Participant*,

We want our account of your concerns and views to be as accurate and as fair as possible. Please read over the summary that follows to see if it a reasonably accurate match with your recollection of the topics raised by you and the other participants. Words in square brackets [like this], have been put in by us to make the view being expressed easier to follow.

If you are satisfied with this account, please just write 'OK' at the end of the last page. If you feel we have missed or misunderstood some important part of your experience or your views on the mental health service, please write a few sentences telling us what we missed out. There is no need to sign your name to this. Please return the pages to (liaison person for group).

Thank you!

*This paragraph was included in all of the summaries.

Five participants, 2 men and 3 women, took part in this group. Individual participants had had a range of experiences of the public and private mental health service at different locations in Ireland and elsewhere. Some participants began using the publicly funded mental health services within the last 3-5 years; others had experience of the service going back to almost two decades. The problems with which participants were seeking help were also various. Consequently between them Group 1 participants were able to give a broadly based view of the service.

Topic 1: Initial Contact with the Publicly Funded Mental Health Service

Participants came into contact with the services in two ways.

A service user who is not in severe distress will go to his/her GP for help. At this point the GP may offer treatment directly or in association with a psychological therapist.

> "Well I...went through my GP...he just diagnosed me. He said 'You are suffering from depression' and he said 'I will put you on an anti-depressant and you can go for counselling'."

Referral to the mental health service occurs if the service user is not improving or has a recurrence of symptoms.

The practitioner might prescribe and refer the person to the (private or public) mental health services at the initial contact.

> "[My GP] gave me [drug named] and suggested I go away to [hospital] for a few weeks rest."

If a service user was seriously upset, s/he might be visited by the GP who arranged admission. The details of this event (however arranged) were blurred but the experience was recalled as traumatic.

> "The GP was my first [contact] and I was terrified like, because you know I didn't have any experience with the psychiatric services....I tore my nightdress because he was looking at me as if I was some kind of wild animal or something...he said nothing to me but he obviously said something to my mother....I

thought I was going to a nursing home and then I realised where I was going and it was very terrifying....I wouldn't go in like and they had to force me in ...."

"My initial contact was through the GP. I went to the psychiatric hospital and my abiding memory is sitting endlessly, I was left there for an hour, two hours and I was pacing up and down this little room, for my initial contact was one of neglect. You know – why weren't they interviewing me? I didn't really know what was happening.... [The participant was admitted on this occasion and goes on to tell of leaving without being discharged] I actually got out of the place and was committed after that. The place kind of freaked me out but I was forcefully taken back and I remember these two big psychiatric nurses taking off my clothes and I had this impulse to just jump out the window. I'm not quite sure why they had to be so brutal but they certainly were...."

"...my first contact was with my GP who over a number of weeks...listened to me and spoke to me but eventually referred me to the hospital and I wasn't given the opportunity of getting a bag ready to take with me. I was just told 'go there' and my parents just obeyed....when I got there...I was just very confused and they wanted me to sign a form for ECT and I didn't know what that was and I don't recall signing it but I must have because they gave me ECT...."

GPs visited in their surgery generally attempted to give the patient information (such as a diagnosis) and some idea of treatment options.

" ...I was given two choices with counselling and medication. ....I wanted to go into hospital and he said 'It is not a good place for you, it is mainly for people who are a danger to themselves, or a danger to you.' He said 'I wouldn't recommend it.'"

"....my GP was not dictatorial, he offered suggestions."

"My GP discussed it [medication] with me and explained to me what it was, but I didn't understand why because I felt weepy and all that and whatever, that tablets were going to make any difference...."

"...my GP was very much telling me what its [medication] effects were and how it affected a neurotransmitter in my brain...."

On admission to hospital, service users were seen by an admitting officer and later by a consultant psychiatrist. Participants emphasised two issues at this contact point.

First although most admitting officers and consultants were noted as being well intentioned, participants found that these clinicians were generally not interested in hearing their story.

"Are you sleeping? Are you eating? and 'How are you feeling?' ....Generally they were the questions. There was no room for discussing things. ...everybody goes into a psychiatric hospital with a story. It is emotional, mental pain of some sort, but the story ends on the first day. Medication begins and pharmaceutical companies take over."

"What he [admitting officer] really wanted to know was, was I hearing voices or was I seeing things...I said I hadn't those problems at all I was just very, very depressed."

"....they asked me if I heard voices and things like that...".

The second issue concerned the absence of discussion of medication.

"But once you went into the hospital that [information on medication and discussion of other treatment options] all went then."

In summary, voluntary contact with GPs was generally satisfactory, although focused strongly on the medical model of illness. The main point mentioned by all participants regarding their initial (and indeed subsequent) contacts with the publicly funded mental health system was the failure of most treating professionals to engage with them as persons. This appeared to apply to both NCHDs and to consultants.

Topic 2: Treatment/Therapy

Participants noted that the only treatment that was always and most readily available was medication. A majority of participants agreed that medication had a place in their treatment regime although it did not offer a complete solution.

"I imagine I would have been much worse without them [tablets] at that stage.....I did feel that [medication did some good] but you know it only took

me so far...I said they are not getting my mood up sufficiently but they are making a difference."

"....I get periods of about 8 months when....I would be fairly [well] but I would say like if it weren't for the medication....I'd probably be in hospital a lot longer."

"...they [clinicians] have given me a very good medication...I am very, very thankful to them...they have discussed it with me and I am very happy with it now."

There was unanimous concern about the issue of over-medication. The following quote is representative of the experience of many participants on this issue.

"...every time I went they put me on a new [medication]....they just said 'Right you are on this as well now.' So they kept adding different tables every time. So I ended up at one stage I was on three mood stabilisers, an anti-depressant and a sleeping tablet."

Participants pointed out that the effect of medication was to sedate them to an extreme degree.

"...it just gives me a kind of a horrible [feeling]. It just forces me to go to sleep. ...I just find the next morning I say 'God I was just knocked out for that time'."

"...like being knocked out and I don't feel the benefit of sleep."

"....they [medication] absolutely

numb, they numb, they turn you into a robot really."

They queried the necessity of having to function in this way.

"….if you are on the right percentage of medicine you don't have to be numbed out completely….".

Clinicians generally did not show interest in hearing about the service user's experience of the medication and working with him/her to achieve a more optimal dosage.

"It [expected improvement following medication] never happened….I said it [to clinician] but they just say - it is kind of ironic really – they kind of say 'You should be doing more things' keeping yourself active and all. That is ironic – they put you on medication and then if it doesn't work they say 'Oh it is because you are not busy enough….'".

A minority of participants did not wish to take medication and were themselves actively working to reduce their drug intake.

"…I am a year off it [names medication 1] now. I am on a low dose of [names medication 2] and reducing at the moment…I miss the [names medication 1] it kept my feelings numb and my head fogged…but my emotions – I never felt with them…"

"It would be wonderful to talk to someone one-to-one with psychotherapy type of therapeutic background rather than a doctor. Obviously let the psychiatrists talk about their medication. That's fine. I see that

as a necessity as well but what I don't see that there can be a contradiction between taking medicine and [other therapies]…"

Non-medical therapies were not uniformly available across the service, and their absence was seen as a major deficiency in the service. The catchment area to which a service user belonged (based on home address) was critical to whether or not the person had access to such options.

"…there is a stark contrast between say [location X] and [location Y]. [location Y] is really top class in comparison…occupational therapy classes…the stay well classes and how to cope with living on the outside, those classes….they had a sports room - a play room they called it. So I am glad I am living in the [names catchment area]."

Even when present these therapies were not necessarily a significant part of a given service user's treatment regime. Occupational therapy (variously defined), art therapy, relaxation sessions, were mentioned as sometimes available.

"There is so little to do like – there would be just a few hours a week…the first time I went there was woodwork…they changed that the last time I was in to every day but really other than that….there was a little bit of art but generally….[nothing]."

"That was terrible – the lock up – you were just walking around…"

"…where I am in [location Z] …they pride themselves in that if you want to talk to somebody they will talk to you and give you a pep talk…"

"Relaxation wasn't there – in the kitchen! In the kitchen! In the kitchen!"

Topic 3: Inpatient Service

Participants who had used the service for a considerable number of years noted some improvement in the interaction between patients and nursing staff.

"They [nurses] talk more about the psychology of what you are going through now than they did 10 years ago…their educational standards are changing as is nursing in every area now….when I went into hospital first a long time ago if you didn't get up in the morning the clothes were pulled off you and the nurses wouldn't be beyond giving you a thump…or I remember once being held down being given an injection ….Whereas nowadays they treat it as though it were an illness like any other illness and you are entitled to sympathy and compassion…".

"Nurses are not as personal [in their remarks about patients] as they used to be…they are more professional in their opinion and they are more careful what they say. That is good for a patient's health and welfare."

However the sense of being imprisoned and of lacking basic rights and personal dignity was still strongly felt.

"…I felt imprisoned…."

"I felt estranged and isolated and lost, you know?"

"We are not criminals, prisoners have more power."

"I felt my dignity was completely gone."

"If you are committed [your] rights as a citizen are waived."

Participants who had experience of both private and publicly funded health services noted a very significant difference between the two types of systems in their approach to service users and the range of therapies available.

"[In the private service] I found the care excellent, the continuity of staff…the cognitive therapy, the stress management classes, the lack of high sedation on admission, the one-to-one availability most of the time and a bit of freedom, a bit of dignity…..[In the public service] the high doses of [named medications] on admission, no choice, label, stigmatised straight away."

"[In the private service] there is an art room and a pottery room and there is a crafts, and there is a stress management [programme] and there is a mood disorder [programme]….[In the public service] it was just one big room and it was all cluttered together and you couldn't focus…."

The absence of opportunities for meaningful pastimes (as opposed to therapy-related activities) was noted as being the general case. One more modern facility has a games room, but this appeared to be part of the occupational therapy system rather than an entertainment facility.

"…there was no real programme at all, you are just left there to think really and another thing I think is they don't encourage [you] to exercise."

The absence of an opportunity to take exercise was mentioned as a particular issue for service users who may stay in hospital for a longer than usual period of time.

"...I said 'Oh God I got no exercise for nearly 8 months.' So it's bad."

"....exercise is very important all right. The garden – I found that very therapeutic."

Privacy in the sense of having private personal space was not mentioned as a major issue in this group. The layout of even the more modern facilities follow the acute hospital ward model with approximately 10 patients sharing a ward. More modern facilities allow Inpatient service users to draw curtains around their bed, and they have their own wardrobe and bedside table for their belongings.

The lack of privacy in performing intimate self-care was remarked upon. Participants understood that patient safety and security might require locks on some doors while others (e.g., lavatories; bathrooms) might not have locks. However, these arrangements are obviously difficult to endure, especially when someone is on the way to recovery.

"...it's basically fine [but] it takes a lot of getting used to when you go in that the toilets aren't closed from a girl's point of view and they are right next to the nurses' station and the doors don't close....they don't lock so you have patients walking in....".

Care attendants were not mentioned by this group.

Contact with other patients was not raised as a major influence for good or ill, although it was evident that some friendships were formed.

Topic 4: Day Hospital Service

The uneven availability of services between health boards and between catchment areas within a given health board came up again here.

"It is very, very good. It is just a great support."

"Art therapy was vital in my first recovery....there is a wonderful art therapist there...there is gardening as well at [named location]."

"They have relaxation classes and there is a counsellor there and two psychiatric nurses...so most of the time if I wanted to talk to someone there would be someone available to me...".

"Location X. But there isn't a lot on there."

"I think they just play cards and games and stuff."

Topic 5: Discharge Procedure

Experiences differed here. In some cases the discharge process went smoothly and included the assurance of support by the unit if needed.

"I have always found it good in all my discharges...I've been given enough medication for one week and an outpatient appointment to follow..."

"And in my last admission...I was told if I need to go back in between that week, just come up and visit ...if you feel it is too much to be out....just those words of support were enough. I didn't need to go back but I found that very nice."

In others it was confused and left the service user without essential supplies of medication.

"They gave me 2 days medication and then they forgot ...to give me a prescription so I ended up with an old prescription and there was changes that weren't in the old prescription ...so I lost out on the changes they made in volume of the two tablets...I found them to be a bit negligent in that matter."

"I said, 'Look if I feel panicky...will there be a change to get in [readmitted]. And he[discharge officer] said 'You rely too much on the hospital service'".

"...I met him [community psychiatric nurse] before I left... [my discharge planning was] very human and very thorough."

"...you know you hand in your personal belongings when you come in and I forgot [to ask for] my keys...so he [taxi man] drove me all the way back....and I ended up paying 17 quid 17 euros because I forgot my keys...they could have got all my belongings together. It wasn't entirely up to me to think of every item that I gave them."

Topic 6: Outpatient Service

Continuity of clinician care was a particular problem in the Outpatient setting.

Service users found this disheartening and disruptive. They felt it led to a situation where no single person had a complete picture of them and their case, and much of the 15 minute consultation period was used up by the clinician reading their notes or the service users themselves describing their problem again.

"...when you come out it is very [difficult to see the consultant]. The registrar is changed every six months."

"...they can't monitor your progress....."

"they take all your details again..."

"you would end up not saying three words to them [about current situation]."

"They hardly make eye contact with you but they are looking at your record and they are so busy trying to find your record....."

Topic 7: Treatment Plan

The concept of a comprehensive treatment plan covering each of the treatments or therapies recommended for a patient, which would be discussed with and explained to the service user and which would have regular reviews of its success or otherwise built in was not part of the service offered to these participants. All participants agreed that the emphasis was on compliance with medication.

"I have always been told you are on medication for life and comply with it."

"….what is their word, it is always comply with your medication."

"I understand what you are saying [about a treatment plan] but no; any part of my treatment [other than medication] would have been my own initiative."

Although the availability of mutual help through groups like GROW; AWARE; RECOVERY; OUT & ABOUT was not suggested to users as a matter of course some clinicians did mention such groups to their patients.

"…funnily enough my psychiatrist….said you could go to Recovery, or GROW or AWARE…."

Main concerns of the group

O Lack of psychotherapists/counsellors.

O Lack of self-power and dignity.

O Basic civil and human rights waived as a committed patient.

O Better preparation for discharge needed.

O Over-reliance on medication.

O Problem of continuity of clinicians, which meant that service users were constantly having to repeat their clinical history.

O Labelling and stigma, which the current mental health care system adds to rather than resolves.

Mental Health Commission Study

Focus Group #2

The views 6 service users - 3 men and 3 women – were obtained. Five participants took part in a focus group and one person who was unable to attend but who wished to give a view on the publicly funded mental health service made a written submission. Individual participants had had a range of experiences of the public and private mental health service in Ireland and elsewhere. They also had experience of the service over a number of years and so were in a position to comment on developments over time.

Topic 1: Initial Contact with the Publicly Funded Mental Health Service

The majority of participants came into contact with the service through their GPs. The latter usually offered a diagnosis and treatment in the form of psychoactive medication, with referral to the mental health services in most cases. This referral could be as an outpatient or as an inpatient. Inpatient referral might then be made by the psychiatrist.

Participants emphasised the importance of the initial contact being positive and hopeful rather than negative and pessimistic.

> "He [GP] drew a big circle and he drew a...small circle and he said, 'The big circle, that's the world and the small circle, that's you.' So I thought that wasn't very nice...I think that the initial [contact]...is very important...it is vital."

> "...no psychiatrist and no GP has ever said to me...they never told me that I can get better - I had

to discover that for myself.... But to have the medical people telling you that [you will not improve/recover] and some of them actually do use the words that 'You have got this for life and you have got to learn to put up with it.' It is just not necessary."

> "...[on] the point of the doctor saying you have this for life; you can't say that because you don't know what caused it really. The person suffering themselves is the only person who knows what caused it. Many people can have their ideas about what contributed to it. You in your heart know what caused it...but you can't have somebody saying to you 'This is for life'..."

This bleak approach created a sense of depression and hopelessness in the service user.

The participants' view on the desirability of a more positive approach was not based on denying the actuality of their experience. They understood that recovery required sustained effort, but felt that it was possible if approached using a variety of therapies and interventions.

> "...I don't believe that any of us can be cured of life 'cause that is what we are talking about but we have got to learn to deal with our emotions...life goes on and we have to learn how to deal with it."

Participants noted that GPs and psychiatrists focused on symptoms rather than them as persons with their own thoughts and feelings about their situation.

> "...the psychiatrists in particular were asking for your family history rather than my thoughts

and feelings that were going on…it was so cold and clinical - all to do with the family history….".

Persons who began to use the mental health service at a young age faced particular difficulties with confidentiality at that point, and this affected their interaction with clinicians.

"… I wanted someone to remove me from the situation I was in and I said it to the doctor….but I was under eighteen. Basically anything I said could be checked up on by my mother so I kind of closed up as soon as I heard that."

The importance of effective intervention at or close to the point of initial contact was noted by the group. Participants felt that this could have prevented problems escalating or become ingrained and thus more difficult to recover from.

"…I have always said down through the years…[if] I would have been taken out of the situation …maybe none of it [illness – would have happened]. Now I am still recovering…."

"After being 20 years [in treatment], being full time on the medication over the last few years I have realised that all my life I have been medicated emotions. …I never learned to [deal with my emotions]…looking back to the past now I do that fleetingly…and then I can get my teeth into it [dealing with emotions]. But nobody else has ever offered me that."

Medication was the usual treatment option offered. Some information was given on side effects, but little or none was given the drug's mode of action and what it was expected to

accomplish for the service user. Participants noted considerable reluctance on the part of their GPs and psychiatrists to discuss their medication with them.

"Just gave the drugs and told to take it…"

"…I would ask the doctors about the side effects and you could see them getting annoyed. It was a case of these are the side effects and we have to state them by law, we have to write them down but you don't really have to worry about them. And I saw one of the side effects was death, and I would worry about that! So I said that to the doctor and he thought I was being smart and I said 'I am not [being smart]. I am genuinely worried about taking these tablets and you could see he was getting annoyed and irritated….I went to another doctor and I went to another chemist and again they were all kind of flippant – 'We have to state them [side effects] by law."

"They [clinician] stated the side effects but they didn't tell me what the drugs would do or anything like that."

One participant suggested a reason for this attitude on the part of medical practitioners and clinicians.

"…they are trying to calm our fears but by surrounding it by so much mystery they develop more fears."

Topic 2: Treatment/Therapy

Medication was the primary form of treatment offered.

"[Treatment is] Definitely drugs based. Totally."

"[There is] a reliance on drugs."

"…medicine was going to be the only solution. That is the only solution that they have to give, basically."

One GP's practice offered a variety of services including counselling, and this practitioner had a very minimalist approach to the use of medication.

"…she [GP] looked at everything and she examined me and all of this and she said 'We can do away with some of this here stuff, you don't need all of this'….She recommended counselling and I am seeing a therapist….".

Participants believed that individual medical professionals are well intentioned. They emphasised that their criticism was not of consultants personally, but of the system which had trained them and the system within which they worked.

"I am not blaming the GPs or the psychiatrists…I believe that it is the system. It is the way they are trained and it is the system that they have to go along with that I feel is greatly at fault. It is nothing personal at all."

The power differential in the relationship between service users and professionals needs to be acknowledged and a more partnership-like approach developed. The apparent disregard for service users' experience with medication was cited as an example of the under-valuing of service users' 'hands on' knowledge of the impact of medication.

"I always had a sort of feeling but never had the words to put on it which I have now because I educated myself to quite a large extent…they [professionals] want all the power and that subsequently disempowers us as patients….Like if you offer a suggestion or ask a question you [are] shot down in flames because obviously I have not had the same education as the doctor, but I have far more hands on experience than he has."

"Several times I have mentioned a certain side effect and she said 'Oh I have never heard of that before' but has still not made a note of it….And I know there is a space in the back of the book to notify the pharmaceutical companies."

The viability of a partnership approach between service users and professionals was raised .

"I think it is a good idea [to have mutual help groups within the mainstream service] but I don't think it would go down well with the people who are running the hospitals because some of our ideas [our] individual ideas wouldn't suit the regime that the psychiatrist is interested in."

"I asked her [psychiatrist] if it would be beneficial if I had counselling and she said 'Oh bloody hell, don't be stupid!' She shut me down."

Participants agreed that medication had a place in the treatment regime and particularly so when someone was in crisis.

"…they have side effects, the tablets I have taken, but I must say they did help me as well."

"I do believe that there is a place, when people are in crisis, for medication…because dreadful suffering goes on when you are either very high or very low, hearing voices or whatever. There is awful suffering and I don't believe in suffering if you can stop it. But [if medication is over-used] I think it is dangerous."

A minority of participants did not wish to take medication and had themselves actively worked reduce or eliminate it.

"For the last 2 years I haven't been on it [medication] at all. But I have had to do that all by myself. By using self help groups – all sorts of support groups – self-help books….whatever is available if I can afford it which is very little but anything that is going free I avail of it."

No participant had been offered individual or group psychological therapy or counselling while using the publicly funded mental health service or either and in- or outpatient basis. This absence of the ready availability of non-pharmacological therapies within the publicly funded mental health service was identified as a major deficiency.

"They never mentioned anything about managing stress or anxiety…"

"…for a counsellor or something – 50 euros an hour is beyond people who are on disability."

Topic 3: Inpatient Service

Participants who had Inpatient experience noted that the needs of the patient were not the main focus of many of the nursing staff. One participant contrasted this with experience of care in a hospital in the UK.

" …you meet some lovely nurses but you are also going to meet people who are putting their day in – that is all they are doing."

"I felt the staff were not respectful to our needs. While trying to go to sleep staff would be talking loudly about their personal lives."

"…I couldn't sleep and I got up and I was just walking down the corridor…but you are told to go back to bed immediately when you are in hospital…and I was annoyed the same night because there was a staff member knitting something…and I said to myself, no, I could do with someone to talk to and this is what the night staff are doing, either having tea or knitting. But I think like the shop and the shop-keeper and the person going in buying something, the patient should come first. Even if it is the middle of the night especially, you are in hospital; you are there for a reason and it is to do with suffering and your suffering does not go away from ten o'clock at night until eight o'clock in the morning….".

"…there was nobody that would stop and talk…I knew somebody that was on the ward and she got up 3 nights in a row, and of course in the middle of the night is when you feel worst. And the nurses- there were two nurses at the nurses' station having a conversation and told her to go back to bed and she was really distressed. Each night they told her. And I suggested that maybe they were having a work discussion. She said no, it was a social discussion and she was in great distress. Now she ended up killing herself a few days later. I am not saying that was the cause obviously but it certainly didn't help."

"There should be more patient care with regard from the nurse to patient and you know you don't walk around the place as if you owned the place....I don't think that is very right at all and the conversation element – chatting and this and that and the other and their midnight cup of tea or coffee is vital and they cannot be disturbed in any way like you know, and that message is loud and clear day-time as well."

"There [in UK] it was great...there is a nurse [available]...if you need to talk."

Participants noted that non-medical care staff were more engaged with patients than were nursing staff.

"...wonderful, they treat you like a nurse should treat you...."

"...she would always ask you how you felt in the morning and I don't think any nurse would ask you how you feel in the morning. Like I am not saying that you might feel good, bad, or indifferent but it is nice to be asked."

Contact between patients was mentioned but not as a major influence, and connection was quite selective.

"[you would talk to] a select few you know?"

Although seen as a safety measure, having to wear night attire rather than one's day clothes was experienced as de-personalising and de-humanising.

"You have to wear your pyjamas because...I suppose they think if you are in your pyjamas you are less inclined to escape."

"You will stay in your nightdress until they decide you are ready to give you your own clothes and nobody wants [to be] walking around in a mixed ward in their nightdress. It is a bit de-humanising."

"It is a big thing ...you get to wear your own clothes again and that feels like home...."

Loss of freedom – as opposed to feeling safe – was an issue. The necessity for security was recognised by participants but they wondered whether it could not be achieved in a less threatening and frightening way than being locked in.

"...there must be another way of doing this. Not a completely open door so that distressed patients can wander around the roads but not a lock up way that takes away the dignity."

One service user explained that knowing the doors would be locked was a deterrent to going to hospital even when feeling suicidal.

"....the actual thought of actually going in didn't actually appeal to me 'cause I couldn't handle the fact that the doors were going to be locked because you see I have always had that if I am somewhere I have got to know that I can leave it. So that was the 'no no' for me – if I had known that I could get out of the hospital I would have went in. It probably sounds silly but I have to be able to get out of anywhere I am at...."

Service users were unanimous in their criticism of the absence of a structure to the Inpatients' day and the absence of activities suited to the intellectual and physical capabilities of patients.

"If there is something like yoga class or aerobics like step aerobics...because you are not physically unwell and you are able. And any kind of physical outlet is very beneficial to you."

"You sit around in a circle...and read the newspaper where the nurse starts off reading her favourite bit...then the next person goes along and reads a paragraph...and the next person will read another paragraph and it is just totally an insult to your intelligence really."

"If you don't smoke and don't like TV there is nothing else to do. That is basically all that happens all day long – smoking and watching TV. And you are basically just walking up and down the corridor...it is just soul-destroying really."

"... occupational therapies...what we were doing in...hospital my 5 and 6-year olds would be bored with!"

"I always seemed to have my psychiatric appointment at the same time as occupational therapy so I could never go...it [OT] wasn't something that they put huge [emphasis on]...".

"We did go to the cinema but I found it mortifying being taken to the cinema by a nurse...to see a group being brought to the cinema is kind of sad because you are losing your dignity and your self-esteem...you would go out of sheer boredom."

The distress caused to service users by aspects of the behaviour of other residents was not appreciated.

"One day while sitting around in the canteen in between meals another patient got sick into the sugar bowl....I became like a child when I was depressed in hospital.. I was unable to speak up...unable to express my needs, and this is all the more reason that staff should be looking out for you (and) protecting you as you would a child[21]."

Topic 4: Day Hospital Service

Participants with experience of the day hospital service spoke highly of it. The attitude of the nursing staff was noted as being positive, engaged, and helpful on a number of fronts from medical to social (e.g., help with career plans etc.)

"There was two permanent nurses...both very nice to me and they were quite good in helping you to look outside as well to new options in terms of career and information and stuff like that."

"I could relate to the staff there…they were all caring. There was no such thing as 'I am staff and you are the patient'. Lively and nice. You could enjoy it."

Other professional services were available.

"…a psychologist that used to visit a couple of times a week but I never saw him…there used to be a financial adviser kind of bloke…I used to see him."

The atmosphere was less institutional.

"You could have a chat and make a cup of tea and cook your lunch…."

"…the sense of freedom - even though it was a test kind of thing…and you had to stay there but the door was open and you went home in the afternoon at 5 0'clock which was great."

The absence of planned leisure and therapeutic activities was still a problem in the Day Hospital as was the absence of 'return to work' opportunities.

"It was quite boring at times, especially in the afternoons."

"I made it clear that I was going out of my mind with boredom which was aggravating the depression and the rest of it. I said 'I need to get back into the workforce. I don't care how I get back into it' I said…and I haven't heard from her [placement officer] since."

Topic 5: Discharge Procedure

There was no formal preparation for discharge.

"Towards the end of my stay in hospital I was told my psychiatrist had said I should spend a weekend at home. This was a very frightening step for me to take and I wanted to talk to my psychiatrist about it. I was told she was gone on holidays….I went on to have a panic attack as a result of that incident."

The more general position was that service users were notified of their likely discharge 3 days before the event. They were not put in contact with community services and mutual help groups in the community as part of the planning of their discharge from care.

Participants noted that staff were careful about ensuring that they had transport to their home.

"They made sure I had a lift…They were concerned that I didn't drive myself because of the medication."

Topic 6: Out Patient Service

In general, service users who did not go to a Day Hospital or those who subsequently finished with the Day Hospital service, experienced a gap in the support available to them from the publicly funded mental health service.

"…I found that [day hospital] very good. It was like a stepping stone between hospital and real life you know. But then once…[that ended there was very little]."

The quality of the community-based support also needs to be improved.

"I would think community nurses are very, very important…they need specialist training for people coming out of a psychiatric ward. …we do know of one particular young woman and all her nurse seems to say to her is 'You have got this for the rest of your life. You just have to put up with it.' It is very dangerous to say that to somebody who has been very sick. They haven't got much hope to begin with [and that] just dashes everything."

The service users in this group used their mutual help organisation to fill this gap.

"I don't have any other outlet or support group. I have no family help or anything like that so this [mutual help group] is the only place for me. As soon as I walk in I can say 'look I feel like shit' and people won't turn away….".

"You can feel the support coming across which is excellent. I never found that with any doctor that I was ever speaking to. They just wanted to know what was wrong [symptoms] and then if they could give you a tablet, well fine…".

"I think it is a type of cognitive behavioural therapy if you like but it doesn't cost you anything."

The needs of people who care for service users also need to be taken into account by the mental health service.

"I lived on my own at the time and my friends were looking after me and they have told me that they would have liked more support at the start of my illness."

Topic 7: Treatment Plan

These participants were not aware of any treatment plans in their individual case.

"…they give you drugs and that is it."

"…there isn't really a plan. They hope you are doing well and progressing but when you come out of hospital they think that if you get more visits back to see your psychiatrist that it would be good for you…I pay [for extra visits] myself."

Main concerns of the group

- More/better listening and understanding of service user's experience and point of view.

- Over-reliance on medication as only form of treatment.

- More free access to a variety of non-pharmacological treatments and services.

- Human concern and caring missing.

- Loss of dignity needs to be corrected.

- Boredom in Inpatient setting and to a lesser extent in Day Hospital.

- Lack of employment opportunities and/or further training/education.

- Partnership between professionals and service users needed.

- Doctors need to be more understanding/less dismissive.

- Ask for and take account of service users' views.

Mental Health Commission Study

Focus Group #3

Six service users, 1 man and 5 women, took part in this group. Individual participants had had a range of experiences of the public and private mental health service in Ireland.

Topic 1: Initial Contact with the Publicly Funded Mental Health Service

The issue of accessing the mental health service is a major one for many service users with anxiety problems. Since fear of public spaces is the issue for these service users, their initial contact with the mental health service may be delayed well beyond the point of onset of their difficulties. This access problem may also affect their ability to avail of non-pharmacological therapies and/or rehabilitation programmes. Participants pointed out that the access issue can be a particular obstacle for rural dwellers.

> "…I remember having appointments with the psychiatrist and I couldn't go to them…"

> "But if I had been living out the country…there is no way I would be able to get [treatment]…I'd be inside in the house all the time. I was just lucky to be centrally located."

> "…[I am living] in the country…I was depending on my [parent] to bring me everywhere."

> "…I used to be crying and getting attacks all the way up the road [to see private counsellor]."

The majority of participants came into contact with the service through their GPs. Participants were concerned that GPs have little or very incomplete knowledge about the nature of the various severe anxiety states. A number of participants noted that their problem was initially misdiagnosed as asthma.

> "…he [GP] wasn't educated [about anxiety states] he had no knowledge about it and no understanding. He did understand how to prescribe medicine…the medication increased each time I went to see him."

> "I don't have an expectation that a doctor is going to cure me, but I do have an expectation that they will educate themselves and know what is there for a common complaint…"

> "…[GP] said she thought it was an asthma attack that I had…"

> "He [GP] was very, very nice to me but …he didn't understand really."

> "After a bit when you kept coming back and …you weren't getting better, with the GP…this is what I found you know 'There is nothing wrong with you [user's name] and I was getting flustered and anxious…they knew nothing about our situation."

They also noted that GPs did not put the problem in context by pointing out how many people experienced it. Consequently participants had felt that they were quite alone in their suffering.

> "I was never told by my GP 'You are normal. That is OK – you will get better…There's lots of people like you out there.' I suppose he didn't know about it either, you know?"

> "It would take away the aloneness if initially you had somebody [who] could have given you all that information you know [that] you are not crazy, you are not insane, you are not on your own…"

While some GPs suggested counselling and reading self-help books, service users were concerned that GPs were generally unaware of the assistance available from mutual help organisations.

> "…from a referral point of view [mutual help group] was never mentioned to me by my GP…I found that [the group] myself…"

The understanding and optimism of psychiatrists specialised in the anxiety states was an enormous relief and boost to the spirits of these service users.

> "Very, very great relief. A fantastic relief…[he said] 'Calm down. I am here for you…' Anyway he reassured me that he would get me better and he did."

Contriwise professionals who took a more impersonal and distant stance had a negative impact on the service user's sense of self and hope.

"You are at rock bottom at that stage…and they are putting you down in the hole completely."

Topic 2: Treatment/Therapy

Medication was the primary form of treatment offered by GPs. Service users were concerned about the addictive properties of the most commonly prescribed medication.

"You relied on it an awful lot."

"They were grand but I was addicted to them…and it was very difficult to get off them."

"You get to a stage that you are afraid to go off it then because you feel '…will I go right back to where I was'…because [of this concern] I am still on it."

The tendency of some GPs to over-medicate and prescribe a number of drugs was also noted.

"My GP…he is a good family doctor, this is not a judgement of him – he just didn't know [about anxiety states]. I would have been on about 16 tablets a day within 3 months and that would have been a cocktail and it took about 3 years [to come off this treatment regime]."

Participants accepted that medication had a definite role to play in the treatment of their condition but it should be just one part of a comprehensive treatment programme.

"So medication, I have very high regard for it and I accept it has a place in recovery. It is just that it is not good enough anymore to hand it out to people without

there being a…proper type of consultation with the other options there [as well]."

They noted that while non-pharmacological interventions were available, the mental health professionals did not appear to be totally clear on what they expected from these kinds of therapies and perhaps did not see them as a key part of the recovery plan for the patient.

"…they [non-pharmacological therapies] were good…but I don't know if the service necessarily know what they are doing …they sort of throw in something and they expect it to suit everybody…and everybody is at different stages…so I don't know if it is taken on board that people are at different stages and sometimes I might have to do something three times to get what I needed out of it…"

The service users' own experience was that recovery required therapeutic action along a number of fronts. Thus carefully monitored medication, individual therapy addressing the deeper personal issues, group therapy, activities such as yoga, relaxation, art therapy, and a variety of occupational therapies, as well as career planning and appropriate education, training and rehabilitative support were the ingredients for recovery or for very significant improvement.

"…for me the medication, one-to-one therapy, group therapy, support groups, combined, work [are effective]."

Many participants had to source and pay for their individual therapy privately and this caused significant financial hardship.

"I wish they would bring therapists into the actual services and allow people the option without having to pay. It is tough enough going through what you are going through without being financially broke as well…"

"If you are not feeling well and you are out of work that is the one time in your life when you have the least income and that's when…medical services are at their most expensive…"

"…I was going to see her privately. That was costing as well. Sure I never had a bean."

The mainstream health and mental health service professionals did not suggest that service users join their relevant mutual help group, and most professionals appeared to be unaware of its existence and its beneficial impact. Involvement with their mutual help group was a major support and the turning point for these participants.

"I was so delighted do you know - I couldn't describe it – so free or something because it was so terrible being on your own like. …But when I heard that other people had it [anxiety]…I actually came out of the room thinking 'Yes – I am going to be better' but I didn't get that from psychiatrists. That group was the only thing…."

"I danced out of there that night! That was the first bit of hope that I ever had."

"…you are made feel so cared for and safe…."

Participants also noted that the nature of severe anxiety could prevent some sufferers accessing even the mutual help group.

"…people couldn't get out to go to the [named group] meeting."

Participants noted that the mutual help organisation's capacity to assist service users was hampered by resource limitations which differed across the country. They felt that the development of the organisation's capacity to provide a comprehensive service on a nation-wide basis would make a significant contribution to the alleviation of the suffering of people experiencing severe levels of anxiety. They felt that while training in the group's programme was necessary, members themselves could run the programme with minimal professional support.

"There are only 2 people doing it [in named location] and they are doing it voluntary…I have offered to go run courses now and they are waiting for funding [for training]."

"I don't think you need a professional [running the group]. I think you can go and do the training and you would be well [able] to do it yourself…it was ourselves that set the group up in [named location] with the back up and support [of professionals] and then the training."

Participants felt a more partnership-like approach was now called for in the delivery of the publicly funded mental health service.

"So really it is down to who is employed in the services, the relationship [between service user and professional] and being treated as an intelligent [person]….It is no longer the psychiatrist is God. We are all here and we all have something to offer that is invaluable. So it is around the services changing their attitude. Pool it [experience, knowledge, insight] together and stop hiding behind their titles as we won't hide behind our being patients."

The importance of having choice with regard to treating professionals was noted. There is no guarantee that the connection between a service user and his/her treating practitioners will be satisfactory. Users of the publicly funded mental health service need to have the same opportunities to change therapists as those in the privately funded sector.

"…she [counsellor/psychologist] wasn't for me at all…I went through a lot of different things before I found the right one."

"I went to a behavioural psychologist and she told me that I was fine. I didn't think I was a bit fine!"

" …and then I found somebody else…I just happened to come across her and she did the business for me…"

"…but if you go in as a [public] patient you are given this person [therapist] and [if] it [the relationship] doesn't work…you are vulnerable."

One participant chose to use non-pharmacological treatments and had ceased taking medication.

"I was lovely and chilled out on them [drugs]… [but] I couldn't work and stuff…I feel I am not functioning on them…like at least before I went on anti-depressants I had emotional highs and lows but when I was on anti-depressants I …had no real highs and no real lows …I went for hypnotherapy [and] I found that fantastic…"

Topic 3: Inpatient Service

Participants who had Inpatient experience noted that the physical layout of the hospital created extreme stress for those suffering with intense anxiety.

"What killed me altogether was with the panic attacks I couldn't cope with people around me, or people behind me. I was put into a ward with 6 people so I would be in bed at night and Oh! like that [looking for air] at a window but there would be 3 others with panic attacks at the same window. God I mean…that is exactly the way it was."

The mixing of service users with a variety of problems was also a source of distress.

"If you are frightened to go out of the house never mind say into an environment that we don't even know and thinking that someone could be mad!"

"…there were people in the ward that did sing and that did shout, great people - some of them turned out to be my best friends – but when you walk in and someone is singing and shouting…they frightened me."

Prior to admission as Inpatients or to attendance at a psychiatric unit on an Outpatient basis, participants noted that they were fearful of other patients, of 'madness' and of 'becoming mad' themselves. One participant described how the staff of the unit to which she was to be admitted invited her to visit it first and reassured her about how she would be treated there.

"…don't put me in there now because I will be only mad if I go in there…today I would go in, but [then] I was so petrified that

I would end up as I thought
['mad']."

"Come in and look if you want
to. Come in and see what the
ward is like….It is not closed.
You don't go round in 'straight
jackets' and you can wear your
clothes….So initially the
warmth…from the nursing staff
[helped]."

*Experienced nursing staff were generally
sympathetic and caring but the approach of
trainee nurses to patients could be inappropriate.*

"I remember an 18 year old
saying 'Come along there [service
user's name]' and doing that
[participant claps hands
together] and saying 'Go to
bed!' They don't have the
experience whereas the nurses
who have been there long term
are lovely."

*The physical condition of the ward and its
furnishings left much to be desired.*

"We used to sit in this day room
and this shitty, smelly, smoky day
room…watching these shitty tele
[programmes] that were so out
of date, with old chess board
games that should have been
thrown out with World War
1…and beside were the tables
where you ate your dinner in this
shitty ward. I say shitty a lot
because I do remember it as
being that…"

"…but the surroundings
now…they were drab, dreary,
frightening really…"

Topic 4: Day Hospital Service

Participants with experience of the day hospital
service spoke highly of it. The attitude of the
nursing staff and of the occupational therapist at
the time was noted as being positive, engaged,
and helpful on a number of fronts from medical
to social (e.g. help with career plans etc.).

"…I have a good experience of
the day hospital…a nurse there
and the occupational therapist
kind of got together, they kind of
took me for a couple of sessions
and it just did so much good. It
was a great relief…they were so
caring."

"I found the day care people
fantastic – they opened doors I
never could have opened at that
stage of my life."

*Participants were particularly appreciative of the
work of the NTDI and its associated services in
helping them to re-train and gain employment.*

"Rehabilitation – especially a
fabulous social worker… and
through them I got a life and a
career…they gave me a
placement [in a position] that
you wouldn't know was
rehabilitation…and they
supported me all the way
through that."

"[Participant enrolled in an NTDI
home-based course] … and I
ended up doing nearly 2 years
then of this based in my own
home…it took me months and
months before I could get up
there to…meet the other
people…and [then] I started
doing my exams up there and
everything….I was coming to the
end [of the course] and I got a
bit of work experience from a

fellow I knew in an office…and I am still working there because he kept me on….[name's NDTI organiser] asked me would I be a tutor …so I have 3 people now that I am going to their homes to tutor them….So everything worked out really well…"

"[NTDI course] Fresh Start…I said…there is no way I could do a course like that because it is 9 – 4.30, and he [education officer] said 'Would you try it for 2 days?'…and then I did the 6 months….There is fierce understanding in there in that particular place. It is a very safe environment…"

Topic 5: Discharge Procedure

Participants who had been Inpatients were discharged to the Day Hospital service. No particular issues were noted with regard to the discharge procedure.

Topic 6: Outpatient Service

The Outpatient service was considered to be unsatisfactory due to the lack of continuity of consultant or NCHD staff. Service users noted that those meeting them on different clinic visits were not familiar with their case. The consultation time was used up with the clinician familiarising him/herself with the service user's history and the service user felt irritated and frustrated by the whole event.

"I just know they didn't read the file….I don't see any benefit in 'How are you, do you want your medication? OK, and how are things?' 'Do you know anything

about me? Have you read my file? No!' So you are not going to [cover] 7 years of work in 15 minutes….I wouldn't have a high regard for the person. I would just say like 'Can I have my prescription?' I wouldn't respect them."

"It is difficult when you meet all these different people [and] you have to…tell it all out again…it gets very, very tiresome to have to explain the same thing…You feel like carrying a tape recorder around with you and just say 'Play that there!'"

"….you got 15 minutes and …your psychiatrist changed and you don't know who you are going to meet behind the curtain."

Topic 7: Treatment Plan

Participants were not aware of there being an integrated treatment plan in their individual case.

"Treatment plan doesn't really exist because…there is nobody holding [an overview of your case] …rehabilitation, there was a treatment plan within that with whoever was in charge of that centre but when you go back to the psychiatric ward there was no sitting down and being constructive and setting up a diary of 'OK over the next few months we try'…In little cliques there was for me a treatment plan but overall no – there was never anyone saying 'Right we are going to do some cognitive therapy and that will work on your behaviour and how you are thinking and then you can have the one to one therapy'..."

Main concerns of the group

- Better information and education for professionals (GPs especially).

- Attitude – needs to be one of equality and respect.

- Treatment plan – a holistic and ongoing approach needed.

- Access to increased public services including counselling, nurse specialists, etc.

- Private counselling/psychotherapy is costly.

- Increased funding for facilities/ groups/ training.

- Medication – needs to be dealt with more sensitively and responsively.

Mental Health Commission Study

Focus Group #4

Seven service users, 3 men and 4 women, took part in this group. Individual participants had had a range of experiences of the public mental health service in Ireland and in the U.K.

Topic 1: Initial Contact with the Publicly Funded Mental Health Service

With the exception of two participants who themselves approached medical personnel for help because they were feeling unwell, participants came into contact with the service when the contact was made by concerned family on their behalf. Some were brought to their family GP. Others were brought to hospital by a family member with GP support and assisted by the Gardai because they were in a particularly distressed state at the time. In all but one instance participants' treatment began in an Inpatient setting. Treatment for one service user began in a day hospital.

Participants noted that they were given little or no information on their situation in any of these circumstances.

> "Nobody explained why I was there [in the Inpatient facility]. I was given medication. ...nobody explained what the medication was, what it was for, or any side effects it might have. It was strange like, and it was my first time in hospital. It was quite strange really."

> "[In the day hospital] I was given medication. I was given little information...it would have been helpful [to have more

information, because] subsequently I stopped taking the medication because I thought I was better. I would have kept taking it [if I had been given more information]."

Participants noted that their psychological state was sometimes such that they did not cooperate with the admittance procedure...

"I didn't cooperate at all because I was kept in against my will. I don't like my freedom being taken away from me and I'd fight. I'd fight anyone who would take my freedom off me."

...and that consequently a sectioned admittance was sometimes necessary.

"It was the only place to be [because] I was out of control. I needed to be stabilised..."

"...I didn't realise how bad I was at the time..."

Notwithstanding the above point, there appeared to be little attempt to prepare or help reluctant service users to adjust to the idea of an Inpatient stay.

"I knew I was unwell but I didn't know what was wrong with me. I went to the GP and ....she said would I go to [local psychiatric facility]. Now I didn't think I was going to be staying there ... I went up.... They [medical personnel] wanted to keep me and I didn't want to stay at all. I didn't cooperate at all but like I signed the form because I was persuaded to sign the voluntary form."

Topic 2: Treatment/Therapy

Medication was the primary form of treatment offered. Service users were concerned about not being given full information on the aims of the medication and any side effects associated with it.

"They didn't explain the side effects either or what it [the medication] was for. I can't remember a lot of that time either. I think it damaged my memory. The first six months I was like a zombie.... There are a lot of side effects like waking [sleep disturbance] and constipation. All these things are affected by it and they don't tell you. ...you are entitled to know really I think. ... they take out the leaflet [information leaflet in package with medication]; either the pharmacist or the doctor does. ...I kept hounding the doctor and eventually I got the information."

"...they should tell you the side effects and they should tell you – in my case anyway - it will take years to adjust to it, do you know?...That you need to persevere with it."

"The medication affects your ability to work."

"My memory isn't great from all the medication."

Participants also noted that medication was of significant help to them...

"Very good, I find it good. More [helpful] than anything else. I had a lot of information first before I went on it...I had read a lot about the possible side effects. So I was kind of ready for it. I was surprised at how it has helped."

...although this was at the cost of the side effects associated with it.

"I put on tons [of weight] but what can you do? It is a side effect of being on the medication. It's like being miserable and depressed or being fat and happy. The lesser of the two evils isn't it? It definitely is!"

All of these service users were concerned about a tendency for health professionals to over-use medication.

"If you start getting depressed over that [contemplating the future] they give you more medication, I mean it is a vicious circle like."

Participants were uncertain about the range of non-pharmacological therapies available and commented that their experience of them was as activities that were generally unstructured and not of noticeable benefit.

"The only one I can remember is relaxation therapy. Breathing and that. [It was] not really useful."

"I think we had relaxation too. But I can't remember."

"Occupational therapy, sheltered workshops. As far as I'm concerned they serve their purpose but they take a long time to do...and the work can be very boring. I think there should be a limit in terms of the time you spend in them and the aim should be to move the

person on. It is a dead end. It is a dead end."

"Psychotherapy. I had that and I didn't find it useful at all.... I didn't get on with the therapist. I felt I was being blamed for everything.... It actually made me feel worse. It was bringing up a lot of stuff that I felt was too much. I mean they said it was bringing up too much stuff so I should just forget about it and I thought, [just forget about it] after dragging it all out!"

"I went to psychotherapy as well...I wasn't capable of deep analysis...it really didn't work out.... I always find with counselling situations like, with one-to-one counselling that the relationship is sort of artificial whereas with the psychiatrist I don't feel that way at all."

Where non-pharmacological therapies were well structured they appeared to be of more use.

"...[group therapy]... in the day hospital [was not helpful]. And the doctor told my mum that I was therapy resistant! But later in [named other location] I was different, [got more benefit]. It [the therapy] was a lot more structured."

The approach of the therapist was noted as important.

"I had art classes. I found it relaxing all right. It took me away from things...[Named art therapist] was a very nice woman, like. She just accepted us and always gave us work to do; and she accepted us..."

Topic 3: Inpatient Service

Communication between service users and medical staff remained distant even after the service users had regained emotional balance.

> "...even direct questioning like; they wouldn't reply. They kind of evade the answer or change the subject."

> "They didn't tell us anything because maybe they thought that we wouldn't be able to handle it."

> "...the doctors I have know ... they are very paternalistic..."

> "I keep hearing the words 'Keep taking the medication.' Most people would hear that....[but] some people need reassurance. They need to be understood because you can be very isolated...and you are dying to tell someone about your problems, like you know?"

> "...the psychiatrist in England...spent about maybe a hour writing down my story...Really going into detail. This is never done [here in Ireland]. ....it's nice to be ...listened to and that."

Participants raised the issue of the degree of care that might or should be offered to service users in the Inpatient or support hostel setting. The risk of institutionalisation associated with being an Inpatient was noted.

> "I was in a locked ward one time and I said, 'This is great...I have a bed, have sheets, I don't have to worry about the world, I can stay here forever.' ...I got used to it then like. Which is dangerous.

> 'cause that wouldn't have been my true character. I was a free person."

Some participants felt that the service disempowered them rather than actively promoting their recovery.

> "They [medical personnel] don't hand the power over to you, like. They take it all away from you."

> "The emphasis should be on getting people back into society rather than keeping them in care. Which is what they tend to do."

> "They [medical doctors] are very paternalistic. One of them - I was in a hostel once and [doctor] said, 'You can stay in here 10, 20, 30 years."

Others pointed out that people differed in the extent to which they needed support in day-to-day living.

> "...some people are scared of society and maybe they want to be sheltered. They want [to be] there [in sheltered living accommodation] for 20 or 30 years."

The group consensus was that the services should offer a variety of living arrangements.

> "People who want to be taken care of should be taken care of and people who want to be brought into society should be enabled to do that."

Safety in the inpatient setting had been an issue for some participants.

> "I found it quite distressing at the time that sometimes police

would drop different inpatients into the clinic and the story would go around that this fellow stabbed someone down town or something like that and it'd make you sleep very uneasy."

"…there was this one woman I used to be afraid of her and in the end she attacked me a few times."

The apparently un-monitored, un-inhibited behaviour of other patients was a cause of unpleasantness and discomfort.

"There was another guy that used to walk around naked in the ward and he used to always spit…and he could be coming right up beside your bed - stone naked – and he would just stand there like…he was just standing there like with fear in his eyes…he was harmless but at the same time…"

"…it was awful because there were people behaving very badly."

Physical conditions and (by implication) staff presentation have improved over the years.

"…the conditions, they were just positively Victorian and it was just filthy. [Over time] there is no comparison because [named location] is gone and even [named location] was a great advance on what was down there."

"The unit had just opened. It was spotlessly clean, the food was lovely…the staff were all well dressed, the nurses [had] lovely clean uniform. The male nurses were nice and clean

too….The hygiene was perfect like. You could have a bath or a shower whenever you wanted and there was always plenty of clean towels. The beds were spotless. The sheets were always changed regularly."

Nursing staff exhibited a variety of approaches to service users. Participants were philosophical about this mixture of positive and negative styles of interacting with them.

"It is difficult to make a judgement when you are paranoid like, but looking back over the years there are some better than others. There are some people not suited to certain jobs…there are some dedicated nurses there like, that who are just made for it. You get some guards aren't meant to be guards. Some nurses aren't supposed to be nurses like; in all different professions [you get a mixture]."

Nurses who were positively viewed were engaged with service users on a footing of equality.

"They took time to talk to you and play cards…"

Participants noted that they and other users with their condition were very vulnerable emotionally and that all professionals in the mental health service needed to appreciate this.

"You are vulnerable like, you are vulnerable."

"You are [vulnerable] and you will be crushed by the slightest thing."

Where a service user did not feel comfortable relating to a particular doctor or therapist, the group felt there should be the possibility to change to someone else.

> "And if you are not getting on with somebody you should at least have the right to go to somebody else with whom you can get on."

> "And say it to them [ask for the change] without them telling you that you are being whatever [critical remark] he said to you."

Privacy during visits from relatives was not easy to ensure.

> "I wanted privacy to talk to my own father and I didn't have that. It was in the ward he was talking to me, like."

Members of the group recalled being concerned about their rights when an Inpatient and when their admission was not a voluntary one.

> "I don't know what rights I had as a patient. I didn't think about that at the time [of admission]. It was only in the later stages I thought about my rights."

> "I was sectioned at the time so again – about rights – I wasn't given my rights either. That is very upsetting."

The opportunity for quietness was rare in some settings but achievable in others.

> "There was lots of people around. And the television would be on all day which I found irritating. I used to try and get away. I would go into the art room if I could. I would ask the nurse. Maybe sometimes a good nurse…would let me into the library or the art room…I would go away for a quiet place."

> "If I wanted to be on my own now I could go off into a quiet room. I could go off for a walk around the grounds around the hospital, walk around the wards and the corridors. Or if I just wanted to lie around and just relax you can draw your curtains around your bed …It [the facility] wasn't too crowded…You could find privacy if you wanted to like, in the [named location]. I don't know [about] any other hospital."

The absence of a spiritual aspect to the Inpatient setting was also noted.

> "I found there was no God up there. There was no spirit…I think that [a spiritual aspect] should be part of [the structure]…like whatever religious belief [a person has] I think it should be supplied as well. Yes, I think that is important too."

> "They never actually asked us if we wanted to go to mass. They probably [thought] we were unwell or we didn't have a belief maybe or something. But it was never asked and I think it should be asked at an interview. Or if you are sick…some questions should be asked in relation to God or spiritual belief or supernatural belief or whatever. I think it is relevant."

> "They had a mass up there alright on a Sunday morning. But they wouldn't tell you about it. You'd have to find out about it through other [people] or the priest. I hardly ever saw the priest …"

The absence of the opportunity for purposeful physical activity was noted by participants.

> "There was nothing on offer to do during the day.... It was just stay in bed or go out into the little garden and look at people playing pitch and putt. It was horrible in there. There was absolutely nothing to do."

The absence of access to a garden or similar area in some treatment settings was noted.

> "No garden. No place to go outside. There is a place that they call it a conservatory but there are no plants, and it is inside as well. You know it is not outside [so there is no] fresh air."

Topic 4: Day Hospital Service

Participants found the day hospital service to lack structure and focus.

> "...they [service staff] were very well meaning. It was not that they didn't care. They were very well meaning but I just found it...sort of very vague. The whole thing was very vague. I would prefer something more structured and more focused."

Participants were particularly appreciative of the work of the NTDI and a similar apparently independently run service in helping them to re-train and gain employment although they did note that:

> "It mightn't suit everyone."

> "I did one of the Fresh Start courses...I found it brilliant. It is a brilliant transition getting from going to psychiatrists or being in hospital....They explore all your career options – anything you have done in your life to date – they will transfer skills over to find something that you want to do..."

> "If you miss up to a certain point they won't let you complete it [the course] which is good in some ways kind of – it kind of makes you go."

> "There is a company.... And what you have is you have a job coach and they go to the employer with you.... They probably tell them [the employer] [about your disability] before you have the interview. So that is a support that is there... They are very friendly and they would do anything for you. They are a definite asset for anyone who has a disability of any kind, ya."

Topic 5: Outpatient Service

Participants discussed readiness for discharge and transfer to a particular aspect of the service (e.g. from Inpatient to day hospital). Group members noted that their 'readiness' for discharge or change of service was not assessed accurately.

> "I think you know when you are ready."

> "They should listen to when you are ready."

> "There's pressure on beds too like. Trying to free up beds. Putting people out before [they are ready]."

The lack of discretion and privacy surrounding the organisation of the Outpatient service was considered to be very unsatisfactory.

"I think it is very wrong the way when you go up as an out patient they call your name out. Your full name and your surname to everybody who is there in the waiting room....If they could have one [a system] where there could be a number...so there is no need to call out your name and address in front of everybody."

"...my neighbour got hold of my one [out patient appointment letter] and it had 'Psychiatric Department' on it and I mean let's face it, the world isn't - the world is very judgmental about things like that. I didn't want my neighbour knowing that I had a psychiatric problem ..."

"There is no dignity. I find they rob you of your dignity very early on."

Attendance at the Outpatient clinic was for medication only. Participants found this regular contact helpful, although they noted one could become dependent on it.

"You just go to the Outpatients for the medication. Every 6 weeks I go back to the hospital for an injection. That is my only contact with the mental health services."

"I find it helpful like, the Outpatients. I had been seen every month for the last nearly 7 years and then last year I was seen every 2 weeks because I was unwell. But you just get very dependent on them..."

Although many participants felt they did not particularly need the support of a community nursing service, they did note that others might find it helpful and necessary.

"Whether you are hearing voices or whether you are insecure and if you can't pay your rent – a whole load of pressures on you – if they [people who felt under pressure] could talk to a social worker or a community psychiatric nurse or something like that. But as for the number of nurses, social workers [it] is very limited and there's such a wide areas that they are usually fire-fighting. You only see them in a crisis, like."

"I have a community health nurse visiting me but I am feeling so well I don't need it now like.... I'm glad that the service is there though for people [who might need it] oh yeah – definitely."

One participant noted that the community care service did not assist with problems that were not directly related to the person's psychiatric state, yet which did affect it because of the pressure associated with the outside worry. Access to such services appeared to be related to the sector of the particular Board where a service user might be living.

"...when it came to...asking for help and it was in very concrete terms I was asking for help with my little boy [did not get the help]. We actually had to change the [location] we came from...[to get help]."

The need for sheltered work in certain circumstances was noted by another participant.

"[I had] a job in the open market, but I couldn't handle it. I needed to be looked after. I needed to be left alone at my own pace like, for a period of about a year. I needed a place where there was no pressure on you, where there was no responsibility and where there was not too much expectation."

"The most important relationships for me were with the social worker and in the workshop the occupational therapist. They were there when I needed support and I knew I could rely on them. So they were a big help in my recovery."

Topic 6: Treatment Plan

Participants were not aware of there being an integrated treatment plan in their individual case. The emphasis was on medication and on getting the dosage correct.

"…there are certain drugs that are on the market for [psychiatric condition] and they will try you on one. If that is not working they will try you on something else and they will vary the dose and they find the right equilibrium - the right medication, the right dose."

"I found my medication gets changed a lot and I am on a lot of different kinds of medication and some of them are counteracting the effect of others. It is a messy cocktail…"

"I have one problem - that I would like to see my medication changed because of the side effects of my medication. And I have said it to the doctors and this is going back about 8 months ago now. And they never changed the medication, [they] said wait…I keep waiting [but] it hasn't happened."

The attitude of consultants and GPs who worked in partnership with the service users and were prepared to discuss medication and modify it in the light of users' feedback was much appreciated.

"I think there is a bit of a change in the attitude…a couple of years ago the last time I went to a clinic, I was contemplating changing my medication because of the side effects…and he actually gave me a choice. 'It's up to you,' he said."

"The GP I have is good. In terms of a treatment plan, a lot of it has been 'we will see if it's working or not working' but at least she is nice about it. …I feel she is very committed, you know? It has taken about 3 years to get the cocktail right for me…and I don't consider that it is totally right, but I think she has been very patient and watched it very closely. It certainly helps [if the clinician is nice]."

Main concerns of the group

O Respect for the service user – common courtesy when meeting (e.g., eye contact; shaking hands etc.) and careful and responsive listening to what the service user had to say would be very desirable.

O Choice – of therapies and activities.

O Confidentiality – use an unmarked car rather than an ambulance or Garda car in the case of involuntary admission.

O 24 hour accessibility to support – the help-line is not always open, but emotional difficulties do not run to a timetable. 'Nobody comes out to you' and reassuring and supportive personal contact would be appreciated at times of difficulty.

O Information – on treatment; medication; illness; entitlements and rights; support services.

O Rehabilitation/community services – should include support for the service users family; there should be easier access to services through a GP.

O Participants expressed concern that service providers such as the Government and the health boards have policy documents setting out these services and so say they are providing them. This is often not the case in fact when a service user tries to access the service. The members of the group feel this issue of contradiction between what is policy 'on paper' and what is actually happening 'on the ground' should be addressed urgently.

Mental Health Commission Study

Focus Group #5

Four service users, all of whom were women, took part in this focus group. They had experienced or were experiencing eating distress. A verbatim transcription of their tape was not possible because of a technical problem with the mini disc recorder. However, it was possible to get an overview of their opinions from the general thrust of the discussion as taped, and from the notes of the moderator and co-moderator.

The technical problem was explained to participants in a letter from the Principal Investigator, and the Discussion Guide was sent in written form with space for them to give the views again in their own words if the so wished. Two members of the group did this.

Subsequently it was possible to obtain the views of 28 persons who visited the organisation's web site where the Discussion Guide was available to site visitors. These persons and the focus group participants had used the public and private mental health service in Ireland. Their experience of the mental health services stretched over a number of years so they were in a position to comment on changes in the type and quality of the service over time. Since the topics covered were similar to those for the 'Independents', respondents to the web site who were not members of the organisation the same questions electronically were very similar, it was decided to treat the views of these individuals as contributions from 'Independents'. Permission to use verbatim quotes from the returned questionnaires was given in all but 2 instances. The cover letter and Discussion Group format are given in Appendices 1 and 2.

Topic 1: Initial Contact with the Publicly Funded Mental Health Service

GPs were the first point of contact and were generally found to be sympathetic to the sufferer, but to have little understanding of the complexity of the condition in either emotional, physical or psychological terms.

The majority of consultant psychiatrists were found to be austere, and despite claiming expertise on the topic of eating disorder, service users found them to be generally uncomprehending of it and of its practical management.

"He left me feeling up-ended."

One participant had a positive initial contact with a consultant whom she was seeing privately. This person used medication sparingly and focused on the emotional and relationship issues that can surround and give rise to problems with eating. This was much appreciated by the service user.

Topic 2: Treatment/Therapy

Participants noted that treatment programmes have improved in recent years. However their therapeutic benefit was often undermined by having too many people rushed through the programe in order to treat as many people as possible. The desire to offer help to those who need it and to run the programmes efficiently is understandable, but participants pointed out that if the required time and input was not given, the sufferer did not fully recover and a 'revolving door' situation was created.

"[Its] better to have 4 [persons] at a time, and do one-to-one and get them better than treat many and have relapse and the revolving door syndrome."

"The relapse rate is very high.

This leads to the revolving door. [I] got worse at each admission – effective help at the beginning is the key."

Participants found one-to-one psychotherapy to be effective. Each of a variety of approaches appears to be useful. As well as non-specific 'psychotherapy', psychoanalytic approaches and cognitive behaviour therapy were mentioned.

The therapy offered needs to be part of a comprehensive programme however. A participant described a very successful outcome of a psychotherapeutic intervention in terms of the insight she gained into her condition. However she still needed a programme to address the behavioural and social aspects of her situation.

Some participants were funding their own therapy.

Creating trust between the service users and those involved in treating them was identified as a key need for a more effective treatment/therapeutic service. Asking sufferers what they felt they could eat and going along with that rather than insisting that they eat what was put before them was identified by some participants as a turning point in their recovery.

In general, including service users with eating disorders in treatment planning, listening to what they have to say and to their insights into their own needs and condition as they experience it would all improve the service to them.

Some participants described a care facility and treatment programme set up privately. The 'partnership' approach involved in this initiative, together with the pleasant physical surroundings of the living accommodation and the surrounding grounds was emphasized as a good model to follow.

Participants acknowledged that manipulative behaviour on the part of sufferers can be part of the condition. However they noted that when this was responded to in a punitive way it reduced their trust in the treatment regime they were being offered.

Members of the group noted that the absence of any programme to help them to deal with difficulties arising from the key part that food plays in daily life is a significant lack in the service. They pointed out that the preparation and consumption of food is a focal point for family, work and social life generally. Service users need assistance in developing strategies for dealing constructively with these settings.

Participants noted that services needed to be designed to suit the needs of young versus adult service users. Therapy groups need to be age appropriate. Mixing pre-teen and teenage children with adults meant that the latter often did not make disclosures that would be therapeutically significant for them, because such disclosures would be inappropriate for young people to hear.

Support from other sufferers who understood the condition from the inside was a major therapeutic resource. Participants identified their support group as a key element in their recovery.

> "It [getting in touch with the support group] was like being able to breathe again."

Treatment – given in the past – that involved medication that increased the service user's appetite was experienced as frightening and was completely unhelpful. Service users explained that increased appetite created through medication, in combination with the fear which a sufferer has of eating anything, creates a situation which is little short of agony.

Participants noted that aspects of treatment that involved insisting that the service user eat the food presented to her was inhumane and cruel.

Topic 3: Inpatient Service

The attitude of very many mental health professionals to persons with eating disorders was experienced as negative, insensitive and condescending. These service users felt that the education of all professional groups on the nature of the condition and on the sensitivity required in relating to sufferers urgently needs attention.

> "Not seeing the person – seeing only the symptoms."

> "[You are a] label, not a person."

> "[You are] stripped of dignity and treated as brainless."

Consultants had the power in the case, but were seldom seen.

Nursing staff and registrars were quite uneducated as to the nature of the condition and their attitude was often found to be rude and inappropriate.

> "[I was admitted at lunch time and didn't feel like eating]. The ward sister said, 'You're going to have to learn to eat sometime, you know?"

> [Student nurse said] "Sure you're heavier than I am!"

The absence of continuity of care is a deficiency in the service. Registrars were constantly being rotated. Those who had no interest in the condition did not even read the service user's file since they [registrars] would be moving on again in a few months time. Those who took an interest and with whom the service user built up a level of trust were also moved on so that the service user was left feeling frustrated and having to start over again with someone new.

The living environment was experienced as completely unsuitable for service users with eating disorders. The range of types of problems on the ward – some people very disturbed which these service users found upsetting for themselves and for their families, especially their children.

One service user described a situation where there was a patient who used to get into other peoples' beds. When this participant's young son was visiting her, she went to her bed to find the other patient in it. This was upsetting for her son and put her in an embarrassing and difficult position.

The accommodation and its surroundings were grim. This was important because the nature of the problem could mean a long Inpatient stay for a service user. One person described being many months in a room with a single bed and a tiled floor, with a grubby and torn curtain on a small dirty window looking onto a car park.

Food was also served publicly which added to the tensions and anxieties these service users were already experiencing in relation to eating.

The food was not particularly palatable or well presented. The focus was on increasing the service user's caloric intake rather than on enticing the service user to come to enjoy food.

Meal times were inflexible.

Topic 4: Day Hospital Service

Participants noted that the day hospital or day centre services offered little support or supervision and this was an extreme contrast with the close supervision they had experienced in the Inpatient setting.

They suggested that a half-way house arrangement, staffed by suitably aware and trained professionals, was necessary to help persons with eating difficulties to make the transition from the Inpatient setting.

The absence of appropriate and accessible support during the transition period, and when fully an Outpatient could lead to some service users 'giving up' and relapsing.

The absence of ongoing professional supervision of psychiatric staff was noted and needs to be corrected.

Topic 5: Out Patient Service

More preparation and support for reintegration into 'ordinary' life following discharge is needed. This point links back to that made under Topic 2 about the role of food preparation and consumption in daily life.

> "No consideration is given to what the person is going home to..."

One member of the group described being given a discharge date and staged preparation for leaving Inpatients and she noted that this was very helpful to her adjustment to outside living.

There is no support given to Outpatients in the publicly funded mental health service, but private services can be more supportive.

Topic 6: Treatment Plan

Participants were not aware of any such plan.

Main concerns of the group

○ The building of trust between service users and the service professionals – it should be a two-way relationship.

○ Continuity of care.

○ A more appropriate Inpatient environment – not mixed in with other types of ailments; better physical surroundings.

○ Change in staff attitude through education. Need for a centre of excellence with appropriately trained staff and facilities.

○ Attention to after-care and service users' skills for dealing with ordinary day-to-day living.

○ Attention to offering age appropriate treatment to service users.

Mental Health Commission Study

Focus Group 6

Three service users, all of whom were women, took part in this group. A man who is associated with the issue of service user advocacy and who is also a service user contacted the researchers to volunteer to give his views. He was interviewed by one of the researchers and his input is included here where its casts further light on the experience of service users. The decision to include this individual interview in this Phase of the project was based on the fact that the service user identified strongly with the group's advocacy focus for improvement in the services.

All service users had experience of the public and private mental health services in this country over a number of decades. They had experience of closed facilities, or closed facilities within more open treatment settings. They were therefore in a position to comment on changes over time and to comment on user experience in the more problematic and difficult service delivery settings. They had experienced or were experiencing a variety of serious psychological problems.

Topic 1: Initial Contact with the Publicly Funded Mental Health Service

Most participants' recollections of the circumstances surrounding their initial contact with the publicly funded mental health services were hazy. They noted that this was partly due to the passage of time and to what they assumed must have been their psychological state at the time of their admission to hospital.

Participants noted that they were given little or no information on the nature of their psychiatric condition and its treatment even after they had regained their emotional balance.

"No, there were no explanations."

"When a person is admitted first maybe they may not want their treatment explained. But as they begin to recover, yes – they do want to know what medication they are taking. They want to know side effects; they want to know why they are taking it; how long they will be taking it."

One participant suggested that easy and non-stigmatising access to community-based mental health services would encourage users to approach the services early in their difficulty and before their problem had become more severe and entrenched.

"That first meeting with the mental health services took so long…. The system has no format for early intervention…if this illness is tackled at the early stages it will not develop into what it does…. I went to my GP and he told me he had no idea of what to do because it wasn't his area…[GP said] I had to go and see a psychiatrist…I didn't want to go near the guy…I had to acknowledge that I was mad. I had to acknowledge that I had a mental illness and I wasn't going to acknowledge that I had something like that because it was stigmatised."

A participant remarked that the needs of an accompanying spouse or other layperson should be taken into account by the system at the time of a service user's admission.

"They left my [spouse] in the hallway of that hospital…and nobody came near her. And she's crying…and she had to get on the train back to [home location]

that night…and nobody put their arms around her, nobody addressed her, nobody came near her…"

Topic 2: Treatment/Therapy

Medication was the only form of treatment that was readily available. This was the case when some participants were first in contact with the services some 30 years ago, and it has not changed in any fundamental way over the intervening years.

These service users were concerned about not being given full information on the aims of the medication and any side effects associated with it.

"I knew nothing about medication at all…we were never told anything about side effects or anything like that."

"You found out [about the side effects of the medication] by something having happened to yourself…you would have a patch or blob or shake or tremor or whatever, and only then - when you complain to the nurse - the doctor would say, 'Oh that's the side effects.' And they dismiss the side effects."

They were also concerned that medical staff were unwilling to discuss their negative reactions to medication and explore alternatives.

"I mean if a drug doesn't agree with you, for God's sake, they should discuss it and be humane about it."

Participants remarked that they learned about their condition and the medication they were prescribed from non-medical sources such as self-help groups and their own research.

> "You learn more from self-help groups than you do from the doctor and the hospital."

> "[Learned about medication] from leaflets and folders. Mostly from having been on it myself."

When considered in the light of participants' quality of life, the benefits of medication were questioned.

> "I suppose Lithium sometimes kept me from going high but it kept me at a low keel. I wasn't reaching my intelligence, creativity and things like that. And whatever dream I had though, life disappeared and it just gets – life's gotten lame."

> "I was on medication for almost 20 years and it just kept me in a zombie state for that time. I was a music teacher…I couldn't learn anything new about what I was good at. I sort of stood still for an awful long time…. I was zonked out…. Like imagine if it happened to you - imagine if all your gifts were taken away from you and all the ways you – the things you enjoyed most in life were all taken away from you!"

> "And some of the drugs can actually make you suicidal…[describes attempt at self injury] [But] I wasn't wanting to die at all!"

[Speaking about the effect of medication on her ability to participate in non-pharmacological therapies one participant said] "Even if it was good therapy you cannot take part in it because you are medicated so much, you see."

Participants who had taken themselves off medication formulated their comments on the impact of medication on their quality of life by contrasting their current un-medicated state with that when they were taking medication.

> "…when you get the freedom of being yourself again it's – the best way I can describe it is it is like getting sight, hearing, everything, having lost them all…even mobility [is] back again. And every day, every day is just terrific! Even though you would have obviously things that wouldn't go always your way, every day is terrific now. I am 4 years now [off medication] and it is just like – freedom."

> "…you feel everything again. You felt nothing then. You wouldn't feel like laughing. You wouldn't feel like crying. You just didn't feel. You wouldn't feel excited. You wouldn't feel."

The role of side effects on the stigmatisation of service users was commented upon in the group.

> "Look at peoples' [with mental illness] eyes. Look at the way they walk…. I used to think that that was mental illness…. But that is how you appear to everybody else…I had a most awful shake for most of my life…."[These signs disappeared when the participant came off her medication].

Participants were not confident that the clinicians caring for them were fully proficient in their understanding and use of medication. They were particularly questioning of the 'cocktail' approach to the use of prescription drugs in their treatment.

"…you might be put on an anti-depressant initially…and when they'd find that wasn't working they would add an antipsychotic to it, then they'd add mood-stabilisers…hypnotics…anti-anxiety drugs and when all of those weren't working they'd add another anti-depressant. So I ended up taking – being on 3 different anti-depressants, 3 anti-psychotics, anti-anxiety, hypnotics and mood stabilisers all at the same time! …You are on uppers and downers and stabilisers so obviously they are all working against one another. It is getting a bit better in that they don't prescribe as many drugs [now], I think. They try to stick to –you know – one or two rather than the eight or nine drugs at the same time."

"I would wake up on a regular basis…with these sort of hallucinatory thoughts. …I thought this was the mental illness and I was going to a psychiatrist telling him this every time. Then I read up after when I got back to myself [felt better] that this [hallucinatory experience] is a side effect of taking the drugs. And he never copped it…like how would somebody who is supposed to be an expert in the field not know that, you know?"

Participants noted that there was no programme for people who wished to stop using prescribed drugs.

"You have to be awful disciplined to get off it [medication] and there are no places for people who have been in psychiatric hospitals to get off the

medication…. I came off Lithium. There were very scary things – like I felt I was going to die and you have to be disciplined enough to keep – to say 'I won't go back.' The temptation is to take it again and to deal with the demons or whatever. The withdrawals are horrific. And the thing is if you are coming off it the only way to do it is on your own. There is no way that your doctor will [assist you] or your GP."

"… if you are an alcoholic there are places where you can go like you know. Some successful place like you know - detoxing…. There are places where – [for] people who go on drugs voluntarily, other drugs. There is nothing for people who are on psychiatric drugs and who want to get off them. And then they make the mistake of coming off them too fast and then it is seen as their illness [rather] than the side effects of coming off medication."

Non-pharmacological therapies were sometimes available in some facilities. Members of the group found some occupational therapy programmes of benefit, although these programmes were in short supply and not available at all in some settings.

"Relaxation with music…that's good. And they do baking or cooking. That's good, that's very good. But there is not enough of it."

"…occupational therapy wouldn't be in all the wards…. I spent over 12 years in a locked ward and there was absolutely nothing. Nothing whatsoever."

The kind and level of occupational therapy available needs to be better matched to the differing stages in treatment...

> "You were so zonked [from medication] you couldn't concentrate on anything. I was doing the simplest things that a child would do and they were hard for me to do."

...and different capacities of service users.

> "Bingo or snakes and ladders. They are an insult to your intelligence!"

> "...so this Thursday we're going to have a quiz. 'Jack and Jill went up the hill to fetch –what?' I don't know where these people [occupational therapists] come from. But it's...outrageous - the insult to your intelligence as to what these people ask you to do in the name of 'Occupational Therapy'".

Participants noted that the uncertain availability of occupational therapy was a source of frustration because service users began to look forward to it and were disappointed when it was suddenly no longer available.

> "They have bits of it [occupational therapy] and it goes grand for a time and you look forward to the next time. Like Yoga was on and I was looking forward to the next week, and [the next week] the girl that was doing it was gone."

> "You'd have something and [it was] great and then it was gone. It's even more frustrating because you have a bit of it and then [it is gone]."

Topic 3: Inpatient Service

Participants focused particularly on their experiences in closed settings in their comments under this heading.

Although the ambiance of Inpatient settings has improved over the years, participants said there was room for further improvement.

> "It was an awful scary place in those days. It is still a scary place to go to..."

> "The physical surroundings might be getting cleaner...everything is clinically clean...there is a man on security [who] lets you in when you are visiting. [The visitors' room is] a small locked room...and sometimes there are 3 sets of visitors there...with no privacy and there's a camera looking down on you..."

Participants recognised the need for special precautions to be taken in the case of some patients in closed settings. They questioned whether such precautions needed to be applied to all.

> "...now some few of the patients...might be [inclined to] violence or self punishing.... So everything is taken off the other patients – lighters, scissors, matches. You are not even allowed a sewing needle. So that you can have no occupation there..."

Communication between service users and staff remained distant even after the service users had regained emotional balance.

> "Well I suppose that [giving information on condition to service users] is changing

gradually in some places, but you know in the majority of places no – your illness is not discussed."

"You certainly don't feel it is a place of care. No way is it a place of care. It is custodial really.... I would like them [staff] to listen to my problem – what I am worried about. What has upset me. Rather than, not only the fact that I am not sleeping, or that I am agitated or something. That is all they concern themselves with – the symptoms but not the cause. And one would expect that after a time in the hospital the cause would be discussed before sending one back out to where the problem originated. But that is what happens – they [service users] are sent back out to where the problem originated and the problem is not fully discussed."

"The man that was the head of the 'round' in the hospital, he just goes round and just says 'Hello' to you and then he has a meeting with them [other members of staff] and that's his way of contacting the patients – through them [other staff]."

This pattern of poor communication of medical staff with the users of their service led the latter to query how they could offer them an appropriate service.

"They don't know you in the first place. He [consultant] never knew me. He never asked me any questions to find out who I was. So how could he diagnose me?"

Although some of the nursing staff spent time

talking with service users, the more usual experience of users was that such staff were distant and disengaged from them.

"And the nurses weren't really a part of your life...they were just there. I can remember one male nurse who – at the time I loved jigsaw puzzles...my husband brought it [puzzle] in and of course I couldn't concentrate on it. The male nurse – he spent all his time making the jigsaw puzzle and he never even brought me in on it...to help me with it..."

"They don't seem to have any kind of feeling for people at all like. I mean really and truly a bit of kindness goes a long way and that's all people need."

"There was the occasional nurse who would listen for a very, very long time and listen a few times, and that's what one needs."

"The young nurses, the student nurses usually [were] good to listen."

The 'key worker' concept was considered to be good but participants noted that it must be allowed to work by making contact with the service users a priority over administrative and routine clinical tasks (such as giving out medication).

"One nurse might have four or five patients with whom she is supposed to chat during the day. But right – you might have a chat with that nurse or you might ask her if you could have a chat and she would tell you, 'I'm busy now' or 'In 5 minutes'...you might get to talk to her and you mightn't get to talk to her at all…they are so busy running here and running there and there's nothing to do but give out drugs and book work…"

The care attendants in one facility were noted as being positive and outgoing in their approach to service users.

"The best people to talk to me were the women coming in to clean the ward. They were the ones that would address you as a human being."

Other patients were identified as a source of support within one facility.

"Other patients – fantastic!"

Participants who had undergone restraint and seclusion experienced them as abusive and horrific.

"When I refuse a drug from the nurse she would say, 'Oh you have to take it…. You are written up for it.' And if I still don't take it I am assaulted by anything up to 5 male and female nurses, put on a bed…and injected with a most painful inter-muscular injection which renders me in the depths of depression."

"…any time you don't comply, or step over the line or whatever, you are punished. That is the system they run."

"…in society like, most things you know are questioned now about that…like even in the classroom like, the children [ask questions]. But we are people…to be treated like this [rights ignored and compliance required]. [We have] no rights at all, yeah. Imagine it!"

"In no other hospital [i.e. general hospital] is one coerced into taking one's medication or drugs but…in the psychiatric hospital if you don't take it you are assaulted…and injected and that is absolutely inhumane and it's a most terrible thing."

One participant considered that a more person-to-person, less custodial approach to someone who is admitted in an extremely distressed state should be tried before restraint and seclusion are resorted to.

"I have seen people come into the hospital especially in [named location]. Bundled in and the person would be talking or shouting…giving out and all this. Nobody spoke. Nobody says 'Take it easy; take it easy, calm down. Have a cup of tea.' No – that's never done. Only hauled in the room, stripped down and injected. That is how they are treated. People who are in trouble! I mean if they weren't in some kind of trouble they wouldn't be there in the first place."

Lack of privacy was experienced as unpleasant and demeaning and this was exacerbated when the nurses made thoughtless comments about the service user in her presence.

"What really got to me as an Inpatient was the total lack of privacy, not even being able to go to the loo on your own…. Having two nurses there when you were having a bath…"

"That was terrible [being observed while bathing] and I can remember them even commenting on [participants physique]. It was terrible."

Participants noted that the absence of activities in the Inpatient setting (whether or not the activities were related to a formal therapy) was anti-therapeutic in its impact on their psychological state.

> "There are no vacuums in life. You are never doing nothing. The mind is always working. So when there is nothing to do and you are cut off from the outside world, you are working on yourself and you are [doing] all this self-analysis. And in my case all that work was negatives – that I can't do this and I can't do that. And that left me powerless."

This absence of constructive activity also led to the 'de-skilling' of service users and increased their difficulties in coping with the demands of daily living once discharged.

> "…I couldn't do my shopping, I can't go to the chemist, my cooking - I can't [do my cooking] and when I came out I was unable to do these simple things…I'm really at home on my own now …and I am not capable of looking after myself. I am still institutionalised."

The negative effects of continuity of care on the contact between doctors and patients and on the clinical management of a patient's condition were a concern.

> "…the same doctor that you might build up – even if they are unfriendly – that you might build up some kind of relationship with…they are changed so often….I had this new doctor … and all he did was prescribe. He didn't listen to me…just prescribed the same drugs that I

was on before and which were really causing me terrible trouble….".

The physical layout of some Inpatient facilities meant that service users might be exposed to the distress of others. This was particularly frightening and upsetting to service users admitted for the first time as an Inpatient.

> "The fella in the bed across the room…jumped up in the bed and started screaming at me…and I just put my head under the covers and I cried. And nobody in that institution came within an asses roar near me, except at tea-time to tell me to get out of the bed and go to the canteen…the indifference of the staff, it was frightful."

Topic 4: Day Hospital Service

The majority of these participants had no direct experience of day hospital services and noted that they were difficult to access and in some cases did not offer a full week service to users.

> "…you have to be referred there and some people might get going – might get there every Monday. Other people might get there every Tuesday so there isn't enough. If you are only going to a day centre on a Monday, what do you do for the rest of the week?"

Topic 5: Outpatient Service

Group members had not had any pre-discharge planning or formal follow up in their case.

"I had to arrange with a friend to collect me."

"They didn't say anybody would call in a day or the next day or anything like that. I had an … an arrangement with a [private] psychotherapist…and I had arranged for one of his psychologists to call that evening, that afternoon. So I wasn't long home when the psychologist came and she was there for the whole evening with me….".

The short duration of the consultation and the lack of any discussion of service users' daily experiences and concerns were noted by the group.

"Two or three minutes…and you are waiting two or three hours for that two or three minutes."

"She didn't ask me how I am getting on or what I'll do with the house or whether I am going to see [family member]. They never ask a question like that. A normal living every day question is not asked."

Poor communication, which continued into the Outpatient setting, could also result in users mistakenly stopping their medication.

"When I would be feeling fairly 'ok' and getting on 'well enough' with life I would suddenly give up the lithium. I didn't realise the drastic effect of going off it suddenly…I ended up back in the hospital ….so that is why they say if you keep taking your medication you will be all right." [But this is never clearly explained to the service user].

The lack of continuity of care in Outpatient settings was commented on.

"And it is very seldom that you would see your consultant at Outpatients' clinics. It is usually a junior doctor and a different doctor each time. No continuity at all."

The need for long-term sheltered living accommodation for some service users was noted.

"…I just don't know when to do what. I am totally and utterly confused…the social worker comes out…once a week and tries to plan for the week for me. But of course she will only plan for one or two things in the day and in between times I don't know what to do….".

Participants emphasised that the approach of those running such accommodation would be crucial to the well being and continuing recovery of service users.

"Of course it is good to have [community mental health] resources [but] the big thing is the regime. The big thing is the authoritarian regime…. That has to change. It has to become – I mean we are supposed to be civilised."

The social work and community nursing services were deemed to be unsatisfactory.

"There was a social worker but…she is really busy. But she is a very nice person and she is as helpful as she can be…."

"I suppose there are a few community psychiatric nurses now that there weren't before [but] you wouldn't see much of them."

One service user was on a community employment scheme that he had arranged himself.

> "Rehabilitation service? None. I'm presently on a community employment scheme but that's only because I applied for it myself."

Support from other members of this and other mutual help groups were identified as an important part of these participants' ability to keep well.

> "[Group member] is a fantastic friend to me. [She] has really worked with me and for me. And not only with me but she does the same for so many others of her friends."

> "There are voluntary organisations – GROW, AWARE, ..."

Topic 6: Treatment Plan

Participants were not aware of there being an integrated treatment plan in their individual case.

One service user commented on the need for such a plan:

> "Did anybody say to me within the mental health system, '[Name] let's sit down and discuss what you should do in the future and how'...did anybody give my wife the dignity again and say 'Let's talk to you madam on how you should care for your husband and yourself?' Because my wife has gone through horrific experiences with this...and nobody gave her the slightest bit of consideration one way or the other."

Topic 7. Service Users As Advocates

Participants had had experience in advocacy on behalf of other service users. They noted that even though a service user might have asked them to accompany him/her at the consultation, the doctor decided whether or not they were permitted to be present.

> "...a person might request that I'd go to their doctor with them or whatever [but] it is basically up to the doctor if they allow me to accompany the person or not."

Mainstream services were somewhat inhospitable and possibly even hostile to service user advocacy.

> "I went to see the psychiatrist because [service user] has a problem getting someone to speak for her. In the beginning [on an earlier occasion] they didn't want to see me at all. Then the last time [subsequent visit]...they weren't going to see me again and I had the Amnesty book with me because in that they say...she [service user] has a right to have someone to speak for her. ...and when I went in to see her [consultant] she had all her students in a room like this...and I was there like to confront her with all this entourage around her...she was making [service user] out to be a bully and she couldn't see that she was a bully herself the way she was treating her [service user]. And she was trying to say as well that she could see our point of view but we couldn't see her point of view..."

Main concerns of the group

- Lack of power and influence over the system – 'We are not criminals.'

- Rights are waived when the person is committed (sectioned). Need to protect individual rights in this situation.

- The system is over-reliant on medication. Insufficient use of other options.

- Labelling is emphasised at the cost of the individual persons particular experiences, needs, and concerns. Emphasis on symptoms rather than on the person's problem.

- Continuity of care from doctors is unsatisfactory.

- Vacuum from lack of therapists/counsellors.

- Public mental health services need to be better planned and structured.

- Discharge procedure needs to be put in place to ensure safety and support for the person while adjusting after hospitalisation.

- Facilities for activities and physical exercise needed.

- The group ended on a positive note saying that it was good their views were being asked.

Mental Health Commission Study

Focus Group #7

The views of 5 service users - 3 men and 2 women – were obtained. Two participants (1 man and 1 woman) identified themselves as 'carers' of persons who were experiencing severe or persistent mental ill health. They were attending this group in order to cope with the stress they were experiencing as a result of their carer role. The 3 other participants were or had been direct recipients of care through the publicly funded mental health services. Some members of this group had experience of private mental health care also, either in their own right or as the carer of someone receiving treatment privately. Participants had experience of care in a number of facilities in Ireland, and one person had had contact with services in the UK.

Topic 1: Initial Contact with the Publicly Funded Mental Health Service

Service users came into contact with the service through their GPs who referred them to a psychiatrist for further assessment and treatment. Two of the service users said their initial contact was positive and helpful.

> "It was a good contact because he [psychiatrist] actually talked to you for a half an hour..."

> "I saw a psychiatrist in [named facility] and she was very good. Because I thought I was going crazy at the time...she just talked about what was going on. I told her and she said, 'I don't think you need to be in hospital. You'll be OK.' Obviously she'd dealt with a lot of people so she must kind of know what she is talking

about. And that really helped me. I think if I hadn't met her...if I hadn't met her and if I hadn't come to Recovery I'd probably be in [hospital] now and wouldn't really be coming out."

The third service user did not have as positive a contact, and felt this was because neither the GP nor the psychiatrist understood the nature of the experience of the condition (panic attacks). This participant noted that the way in which the condition is conceptualised in the programme of the mutual help group (as 'Air Hunger') was useful to him in coming to terms with the problem and coping with it.

"I was...diagnosed by my own GP, that this is exactly what it was.... But...it was a thing that he couldn't kind of get it across...I think the thing was, he was kind of looking at it as a triviality, where I was looking at it as a dire or emergency kind of thing."

"I felt he [psychiatrist] saw [only] one side of it...we couldn't kind of get a middle ground because what I was kind of suffering from to me was very, very fearful...and basically I felt that he hadn't a clue [how frightening it was]. I remember sitting with him and he said to me, 'You know if you just hold your breath you will see that you can actually breathe.' But when you get into a situation where you feel that you can't get your breath...that to me was something [frightening]...you know, if they just said, you know...I accept what you're telling me..."

The self-identified carers in the group had somewhat different initial experiences. In one case the family member was an adult with a severe or persistent mental health problem. The initial contact with the mental health service was arranged by the family member's (non-psychiatric) medical consultant. The admission was to a private facility. Specific information on the service user's condition appears not to have been given or sought.

"And she was kind of sedated if you like for about 10 days nearly...and she'd have these kind of little blips and that...and I'd ring up the hospital and the doctor would say, 'Well, Mr. [carer's surname] she's going to have these little things, you know?" And they'd say 'Well just increase the medication'."

The second carer sought help for her son who was unable to settle at school and who was developing behavioural problems. The carer was dissatisfied with the quality of the psychiatric assessment carried out and the 3 year long delay before a psychological assessment would be carried out.

"I took him to a psychiatrist. ...and I wasn't that happy with him because he just started firing a load of pages at me 'Go home and read them, go home and read them...' and started saying, 'I'll put him on this and that' without really chatting to the kid or hardly seeing him at all – just talking to me.... And I was on to the health board and they said you'd have to wait another 3 years. And I couldn't wait 3 years with that kid because he was failing in schools and he was being very stressed at home and the anxiety for me was very difficult.... In the end I had to go to England at enormous expense to get him the help and the diagnosis there. And that's what people have had to do you know?"

The carer described the experience in the UK to support her dissatisfaction with Irish services in this area.

"The doctor sat down and he listened very carefully to what I had been through with the kid. And he talked to the kid...the psychologist assessed him [son] as well and it went on for a couple of hours you know?"

Topic 2: Treatment/Therapy

Medication was the primary form of treatment offered within the mental health care system.

"They tend to [ask] 'How are you? How are you feeling today? Is your appetite good? Are you sleeping well?' You know, four or five standard questions and you're in and out in 5 minutes.... You get the prescription at the end of it – [or rather] you don't get a prescription anymore. You have to go to your own doctor for the prescription. It's a standard prescription."

Both service users and carers saw medication as necessary elements in treatment, although their views were mixed and in some cases uncertain on the value of this approach when considered in terms of possible side effects and impact on quality of life.

"I take it diligently, you know? But I don't know whether it works or not because I just take it. I still get ill. So I go up and I go down, so the medication has

no effect. It has an effect but I don't know whether it has an effect.... It's a sort of insurance policy."

"Just from the carer's side, I could see the effect on [family member] if she doesn't take medication and it's generally not good. If she hasn't been taking medication, she can't sleep at night; she becomes restless and so she becomes slightly delusional.... I would perceive the medication as a necessary thing."

"...there's a lot of side effects there that you worry about and have to think about. [Drug] was good to a point but it sedated the kid...he was dull from it and he would have been very bright and playful – [a] dramatic kind of kid and it deadened him totally. He was just like a zombie really. But he was quiet and good in school .... But now it's very difficult now that he is off medication...you know, despite the side effects of [drug] the teacher even said that if he stayed on it just to get through his Leaving Cert. he'd be older and more mature then..."

One service user spoke appreciatively about the partnership approach of his GP to managing his medication.

"He had me on it [drug] for a while...we discussed it and he then started to reduce it. And eventually I came off it onto something else. And eventually I'm down now [to a low level on substitute medication]. I do take medication...but I must say that I was very pleased with my own

GP because he actually brought me down…[reduced dosage significantly].”

Another service user noted with appreciation that the consultant had arranged for him to go out to his job each day from the hospital where he was receiving drug treatment.

"…I will say on a positive note, my former psychiatrist …the last time I had the depression and was in, she actually sent me back to work from the hospital. Like that was positive.”

Service users and carers who wished to access non-pharmacological treatment/therapy noted that they funded this themselves.

"…if I want to get a bit of psychotherapy like I go to a psychotherapist privately…because I don't think I get that from the health service…”

"My other son was attending a psychiatrist because they thought he was depressed but I think that it was the stress at home…[son] was in counselling for a good bit but that was privately as well. It was private as well because we couldn't wait.”

The benefits of non-pharmacological therapies were variable.

"I went and I did TM for a while…it absolutely did nothing for me, you know? {Service user then tried hypnosis}…I had 3 sessions…he [Hypnotherapist] said at the end of the 3 sessions…I wasn't a candidate for hypnosis.”

"It [counselling] was very good

for him at the time and the whole family.”

"I've gone to a psychologist privately and he's useful.”

The quality of delivery of these non-pharmacological services varied across therapists.

"I went to a counsellor and after about 5 minutes they told me I knew it all! I couldn't believe it! I subsequently went to another counsellor. It was the best thing I did. There was kind of 3 sessions and I kind of told my story and they [two counsellors were involved on this occasion] gave me feedback. Then they came up with a plan…. So that was a good experience.”

"…and after the second appearance with the psychologist she said I was fine…I was better. They had solved my problem…but I mean…I'm Bipolar…I've had the illness for 30 years…”

The programme offered by their mutual help group was useful to all participants. It seems that the members of this mutual help organisation find that its programme goes a long way towards fulfiling their needs for a non-pharmacological therapeutic strategy.

"[After a reassuring consultation with psychiatrist] I started the road of kind of doing it for myself. I found [organisation] on the doctor's notice board in the Community Centre. It [group] was very warm and welcoming and the people were very good there - great. The people understand what you're going through so you don't feel that you're on your own.”

"I was able to identify with the people that were actually on the [TV] programme [about benefits of support group] – what they were talking about. And as well as that it [group's meetings and programme] was very well structured...."

"I [carer] found that I was suffering a bit of anxiety myself about it [family member's ailment] and it [group programme] worked. You learn these methods and I got insight into what was going on...it's been a great help to me."

One service user had devised a satisfactory treatment regime based on combining medication with use of the mutual help group's programme.

"I use [Group] to function during the periods when I'm down or depressed and I work away. ... I've kept my job for 28 years. [When I am high] I go to hospital because I don't get prior notice. ...they've talked of manic depressives...who know when they are going high and [can] counteract it.... I don't normally know...my kids would tell me that I was sick. But then I'd go to hospital and then I'm recovered in a few days."

The GP in one case was encouraging and supportive of the service user's active membership of the mutual help group.

"He is a big believer [in the group's benefit to the service user]...he always says to me that 'You're doing well.' It's great to have that type of relationship with your GP, you know?"

Participants felt that consultants should make more use of mutual help groups as adjuncts to their use of medication or other more formal therapies in their care of service users.

"There's a reluctance as well among the psychiatrists to refer people to places like [support group]. Very few people are actually told about [group] and there's actual research that was done in the States that shows that people who come regularly to [group], they cut their dependence on the health services by about 50%."

"The main thing about [group] – we've been trying to get this across for a long, long time – is that we don't [do] doctors' jobs, we're not qualified, we don't diagnose for people, we don't talk about medication at the meetings. What we're actually trying to say to them [medical professions] is that, 'look – we can work in parallel with you.' You might be over-run with patients...and like here's a self-help group that is willing to invite people.... We just want to work in parallel with them."

Participants speculated that the almost exclusive reliance of consultants on medication and their relative non-involvement with service users in other ways might be the result of the under-resourcing of the mental health system.

"The only thing that I can excuse them would be that maybe that they're so swamped. If you're so swamped with work you're just kind of hanging on by the skin of your teeth all the time."

Topic 3: Inpatient Service

A participant who had Inpatient experience of public and private facilities and of open and closed wards, noted that the experience of the latter was the same across both types of funding arrangements.

> "It was the same as everywhere else."

On open wards in publicly funded facilities, interaction with staff was minimal both in terms of duration and depth of contact.

> "There's no or very little interaction between the nurse and the patients. The…nurses tend to stay in their office and chat away…. They do the beds or whatever they have to do but they don't tend to interact with the patients. You'll see the doctor for your two or three minutes once every four days, every three or four days."

> "…you know the way you actually see a general nurse – [s/he] will actually look after you. They've [psychiatric nurses] got so used to the idea that you can do nothing for these patients that they've developed…they don't take much interest in you."

In the publicly funded sector Occupational and other therapies were poorly organised and of poor quality. In some cases they were delivered by persons not trained in the specialty.

> "Newspaper reading for half and hour. They have Bingo and things like that. They have relaxation tapes and they do a bit of cookery some days…and they have a bit of timber work. But do you see, there's only room for a certain number of people [at these activities]."

> "…it lasted for about half an hour and they read the horoscopes. You know…when you think about it as a way of getting people out of themselves, it's not that great, you know?"

> "The people who run the occupational therapy were nurses…"

There was a general absence of ordinary recreational activities which could have been of therapeutic value.

> "You're sitting around on your own usually…most people would be depressed so they're not very talkative to each other. They sit in watching – the television is on all day."

> "People just sat and watched television. You might as well have been looking at the wall. That is my opinion of it."

In terms of resources, Inpatient services have deteriorated over the years.

> "It's happened to me a few times that I've been actually sent home because I was the best patient on the ward. I was sent home from the ward but not discharged from hospital. I was sent home as a patient…to sleep at home…to go back in the morning…. Because they had to do it…they had no bed for someone coming in."

> "I think it's got worse after '87 because I can remember…there used to be a dance on every

Wednesday – playing music and a bit of craic but that's all gone. And they put up plants and everything – the whole thing – and they're all gone."

Service users questioned whether safe and easy access to grounds or gardens was given sufficient priority by service planners.

"…you're supposed to get permission to go off the premises but you can go for a walk around the building [indoors]. Now I'm not sure what the situation would be in [other facility] because there is no grounds attached."

Participants who had experience of Inpatient services noted that placing persons at different stages of recovery in the same wards or sitting rooms of a facility was disturbing and not therapeutic for those who were further along in their recovery.

"There's no streaming of patients, you know? I could be well and I'm among…patients who are not well."

Service user participants identified training as a key area for action if the Inpatient experience was to be made more beneficial to service users generally.

"They [medical personnel] all belong to the same [organisation]…. They started from the same group. They come from that group. They've learned all the habits of the system, the bad habits."

One of the carers felt that the range of activities available to users of privately funded services have improved rather than deteriorated. Since this participant did not have Inpatient experience

we simply note this as something to examine at another time.

The relative infrequency of medical rounds could have a negative impact on the quality of service received by the user.

"I'd been in at Christmas and I should have been [discharged] on the third day but because there was no one [doctor] coming in, I couldn't get out."

Difficulty in accessing services outside daytime working hours was noted. Although the participant acknowledged that admission through the A & E department of the general hospital could be sought, the point being made was that persons who are unwell may not think about this option and may simply go to the psychiatric facility with which they are familiar.

"There was one night I arrived up at the hospital to admit myself and the guy knew I was sick. They wouldn't let me in…they sent me home. And the reason why they didn't want to let me in was because they'd have to…get a doctor…do all sorts of things and it was the middle of the night…that just to me shows the attitude, you know?"

Topic 4: Day Hospital Service

These services were considered to be inadequate owing to lack of structure.

> "Again it was unstructured, it wasn't well organised. You just had the dinner in the middle of the day. That's the only certainty you had each day."

Topic 5: Discharge Procedure

The members of this group did not raise particular issues under this heading.

Topic 6: Outpatient Service

Lack of continuity of care in the Outpatient setting was noted as a deficiency in the services.

> "I never see the same doctor twice…you have no continuity so it is like starting over again every time."

> "Well, I don't know who it is [service user does not know which doctor is their consultant]."

> "In terms of Outpatients…you've no guarantee of meeting the same psychiatrist or the same SHO even."

The organisation of Outpatient medical services allowed no time for a significant non-pharmacological therapeutic input.

> "It's [psychotherapy] not available because they don't have the time. Because you actually arrive in and there's 20 people in front of you and they're all down for half nine in the morning…"

> "There's no time. I mean people who haven't been in the system don't realise how little time is actually given to people. I mean you have about 40 patients between about half nine and twelve o'clock."

Day centre services were described as poorly structured and unplanned.

> "…there was about 30 people there…and you could go a whole day without talking to anybody. I would have found that it wasn't very well structured anyway."

Social work and other community-based interventions were inadequate.

> "Social workers only come in when things are gone really bad. They don't come in earlier. They come in when it's too late and then we're really in trouble."

Members suggested a role for the community nurse in primary care and in- and Outpatient settings who would act as a liaison and source of information between the service user and relevant community-based services and organisations.

> "If there was a community nurse with a GP and if she kind of interviewed the patient and if there was any kind of problem…she would be able to refer them to the appropriate [service] from there on."

> "That would be helpful in the Outpatients' situation."

> "In the Inpatients system as well…."

The need for State support services to be able to accommodate various service users in the impact of mental health problems on their capacity to work was noted as an area for action. A self-employed service user described the difficulties facing someone who may need to work in non-typical ways (e.g., occasional work; part-time work; supported work).

"[because] I'm on medication I wouldn't work as fast as other people…if I go to my accountant and tell him that's what I earned for the year and he looks at me and says 'You couldn't survive on that.' And I have to go through a big litany with him because I'm on this and that and can't work as fast as another guy. And it's like the red tape attached. Because he says 'If I sent that into the Revenue they're going to be asking questions as well.' And they have – what medication I'm taking and so on. And you still have to go through it every time. And it's hardship…actually you could get very anxious. Your anxiety level could go way up from it. What I'm talking about is that I'm just [caught in] the middle of the road – I could pack up work and go on Disability which I don't want to do. I want to stay working. [The system] doesn't want to deal with it [the person who needs some support but can also make a contribution by continuing to work to some degree]…I think there's an awful lot of people in that situation."

Inadequate communication between elements of the health system had created a problem for one participant who noted this as an important area for future action.

"…just having a normal hernia operation. …when I 'came to' I was brought back down to the ward. The thing was I was perspiring like mad…I was fine because I knew what was happening. The night previous to the operation I had no [psychotropic] medication…and …I was actually in a situation where I was going into a panic and I was trying to tell them. The thing was that I was getting oxygen and I didn't need oxygen! There was no mention of medication in fact [when preparing for the operation]. Two days later when they came around with the medication…it was a different dosage…. And the thing was that I went into a panic because I felt that I was actually going to go into a panic because of this."

This participant also expressed concern that the stigma attached to mental ill health can influence the care offered in general hospitals for non-psychiatric conditions.

"…the actual surgeon came in…he just said to me, 'Who is at home if you went home?' …I couldn't read his mind [but] what I felt was that – I think he wanted me out of the hospital…I was only after having an operation! …people that I had known who would have had operations would normally be in for maybe four days…. I got the impression…that they felt that if your man gets a massive panic attack here you [he] may not want to leave, kind of thing!"

This participant suggested that there should be someone within each general hospital who would look after issues that were not directly related to the ailment for which the person was admitted.

"...there should be someone in the general hospital...in case...in the situation where somebody comes in who suffers from, as I say, my anxiety kind of situation."

A carer noted a similar need for better liaison between health and education services.

"Certainly Education and Health I think need to come together somewhere to help young people...these years are very important when they're small...because at the end of the day...that [absence of effective intervention] effects them [children] psychologically and it [can] end up in suicide."

Topic 7: Treatment Plan

Participants felt that there probably was a coherent treatment plan for medication.

"...she [consultant] said we'd try this level...they ask me about it [review its impact]. It seems like the actual level I'm on is the level I should be on...."

"...and he [GP] said 'If you feel that [is] a bit strong we can always bring it down.' We work together and I can ring him and ask him."

The issue of treatment plans for other types of interventions did not arise since these were effectively non-existent within the publicly funded health service as experienced by these participants.

Main concerns of the group

○ More 'caring' in patient care. Mental health professionals are generally experienced as being distant from service users and uninterested in them as persons.

○ Better communication between state systems to ensure a better, more coherent, and safer overall service. For example, the Departments of Health and Children and Education need to coordinate their services so that people (like school children) who need cross-disciplinary intervention can get it. Communication between the mental health system and the general hospital system needs to be better coordinated so that a person using the services of both can be assured of good and safe care.

○ Need for community nurses to assess service users' needs and act as liaison between them and available services at primary care, Inpatient and Outpatient levels.

○ Outpatient system needs to be reorganised. There is no continuity of the relationship between service users and their consultants. There is insufficient time for people – to listen to their concerns and work with them in a therapeutic way.

○ Lack of resources in the publicly funded mental health system. Pressure on beds in Inpatient facilities; insufficient numbers of properly qualified and trained staff to ensure therapeutic interaction (e.g., qualified Occupational

Therapists; properly designed and structured programmes in Inpatient settings, in day hospitals and day centre).

○ Need for referral of service users to self-help groups by professionals.

○ There is no service to young people so that difficulties can be identified and resolved before they become entrenched problems. There is a need to train teachers, social workers and others interacting with young people to identify problems so that early intervention can take place. Obviously such early intervention services need to be readily available and accessible.

Mental Health Commission Study

Focus Group 8

There were 7 participants, 4 men and 3 women, in this group. All were carers of family members who were or had been experiencing significant psychological and psychiatric disturbance. Individual participants had had a range of experiences of the public mental health service in Ireland and the U.K.

Topic 1: Initial Contact with the Publicly Funded Mental Health Service

Carers contacted the service through their GP when they noticed their family member becoming unwell or behaving erratically. The GP was identified as a key person in the carers' attempts to access the service.

> "…he [GP] was the guy you depend on to take you seriously."

> "…to get a section you have to get your GP's support. For your GP to make a diagnosis you have to get the patient to the GP. How do you get somebody who thinks there's nothing wrong with them to the GP?…he [GP] listened to me. I was lucky with my GP. Very, very [lucky]. …I had GP support, number one. Without which you're nowhere because that person [family member] was over age."

GPs varied in their knowledge of serious psychiatric disorders as well as in their understanding of its treatment and their ability to communicate the nature of the problem clearly to the carer.

"[Named GP] he was absolutely wonderful. His diagnosis to me was that [family member] had a thought disorder." {This practitioner then seemed to explain 'thought disorder' to the carer in terms of the behaviour of the service user}.

"We would have mixed views about how adequate he [GP] was in the whole situation…he diagnosed…but didn't give us any what we regarded as useful advice on how to cope with it. No information. No advice. Well, our GP's advice was you know 'Make [family member] face up to reality', you know, 'push him out on his own and leave him there', you know? Which we didn't do thankfully…as the illness got more severe and acute…"

Communication with other professionals was not satisfactory either. This inadequacy in the service related both to how the information was given as well as to the clarity and helpfulness of the content of the information.

With regard to being given a diagnostic label without further clarification in practical, day-to-day living terms, participants said the following:

"Because being told that you have schizophrenia or being told that your family member has it doesn't advance anything."

"[GP referred us] to a consultant who gave us – very rapidly – a diagnosis…[consultant] had absolutely no concept about how to give that information to the family. And [was] unable to convey the concept to the patient…the prognosis [which the consultant] gave turned out

to be inaccurate…in retrospect I think none of us realised until it was too late how dangerous [consultant's suggestions regarding the service user] was for [family member]…."

Instances of inappropriate and insensitive styles of communicating with carers were noted by the group:

"And [psychologist/psychotherapist] said there's nothing wrong with him. There's something wrong with the two of you [parents]. And a week later [family member] was in hospital."

"The first time I actually got [family member] up in [named psychiatric facility] the consultant told me what the diagnosis was and said, 'I think I would rather be telling you that [family member] has AIDS.' And [that] was a top consultant! Oh ya!"

Carers feel quite unsupported in this initial phase of their contact with the publicly funded mental health services.

"Given [family member's] case history it was incredibly dangerous and as far as we know there were no support services at all…."

"…the worst thing I ever had to do in my entire life [was arrange a sectioned admittance]. I had to get a little thing from the doctor saying that 'Yes' [family member should be admitted]. Then I had to call the police. There was nobody, I was alone. I had to go and knock on my [family member's] door and get him to come with me to the hospital….The Judas at the door. You are waiting maybe 2 – 3 hours to see a consultant…and it being the way it is [shortage of beds] they will not admit somebody unless they feel it's [essential]. So I was praying he would be as crazy as possible in front of the doctor. …you can imagine being disloyal [to your family member] and nobody from the Social Services there in any shape or form to support you."

Carers felt that their views of a service user's need, based on their experience of that person, were not given proper weight at this stage of initial contact. This was a theme that came up repeatedly as each topic was discussed.

"If somebody came in – [if] a friend of mine came in they would go home saying that there's absolutely nothing wrong with [family member] whatsoever. And they [family member] can do that in front of the doctors…. I had to get my [family member] to argue, you know, for it [psychiatric state] to be seen."

"The problem is that they [mental health professionals] don't listen to the parents and relatives sufficiently. They completely underestimate the value of the relative's appraisal of the situation. Even though it may be a lay appraisal it is a very intimate knowledge that they possess. And these guys [professionals] tend to…they totally disregard a lot…."

Topic 2: Treatment/Therapy

Participants acknowledged that medication to stabilise a service users psychiatric state was often

necessary, but they emphasised that this should be a step on the way to a more comprehensive programme of treatment/therapy.

"…get [service user] somewhat stable, in a condition that you can then be receptive to some of the information [on the condition and on medication]."

"It is not just medication that helps somebody…. There's also your self-esteem, there's confidence, there's coming back to reality after being away from it for a very long time because their mind doesn't work the way our minds work."

"There's no therapy group and life skills and how…on getting [service user] to come to terms actually with [the] diagnosis and [the] illness and to start to manage that himself. [There is] absolutely nothing at all about how to manage yourself, taking medication or whatever else…."

Participants cited examples of improvement where therapies other than medication were used, and felt that these and other more speculative options such as attention to diet should be part of the treatment approach.

[Speaking of a Cognitive Behavioural therapist employed by health board]. "The difference that he made to my son cannot be told…. At the start I thought it [CBT] won't work at all…he would talk to [family member]. He'd talk him around and he'd say 'You can…'and he'd make him feel that it wasn't this terrible thing that he [family member] thought it was."

"[Professionals say there is] No cure! But then you have people like my [family member] who has chosen to come off the medication. He is still a schizophrenic. He still has his thoughts. He still has his moments. But he has got to a stage through – with me helping him, he could actually live alone."

"There is an area that is quite important in the cause of this illness and it is diet. All the focus of treatment in the mainstream psychiatric services is on manipulating the Dopamine and the Serotonin or whatever it is, and all the rest. But actually there's another area - is the deficiencies of essential fatty acids."

In the experience of these participants other therapeutic options were difficult or impossible to access.

"There is [counselling] but we can't get it."

"We won't get it because it – they decided that it is not appropriate, that [service user] won't respond to it…we are doing it privately now. But through the services we are being denied completely."

"I was told the same…[access to alternatives to medication denied]."

*One participant told of accessing a suitable service through the **probation** system.*

"What is ironic…he was on probation. The probation service run a course for 2? days a week which is absolutely ideal for his condition, because it is very supported, they run discussion groups etc. That wasn't available

through any other source we were aware of."

The under-valuing of the experience-based judgement of the carers in relation to a service user's readiness for therapies other than medication was noted.

"We think he's ready for it now, yeah. And he's prepared to go along with it now whereas previously he wouldn't speak to people you know."

Psychiatry's 'gate keeping' role vis a vis carers' contact with other mental health professionals was commented on.

"If you want to see the psychologist who is working on the therapy – behavioural – side with your child on the Outpatient or when they are in hospital, you have to first go through …the consultant and ask [their] permission because if you go direct to [psychologist] then it is all politics. So you have to get [consultant] to say, 'Yes, it is ok for you to speak to [psychologist].' Or else he [psychologist] gets into trouble and stuff."

"…it's through thick and thin and trial and error that you find out that there is a psychologist there in the first place, do you know what I mean? Unless you are a conscientious parent or family member helping that person in hospital, there is nothing – no information coming to you from them. You have to go looking."

The team approach experienced by one carer whose family member is an Inpatient in the UK was contrasted with the service structures in Ireland.

"There's a team now. He has full time psychiatric nurses… He has a consultant, a psychologist who is working on him on behavioural – cognitive behavioural therapy and helping him recognise the onset of the episodes and what to look for, the triggers and stress and what have you. There's a social worker…there's just this lovely team of people and they have meetings around him."

"…with our medical services in Ireland they'll talk about multi-disciplinary teams in Ireland but exactly in what way [do] they actually function? Because everything is aspirational in Ireland."

"All aspirations and no performance!"

Topic 3: Inpatient Service

The admission process can still be 'too forceful' where a service user is distressed at the time of admission. This it upsetting to the carer and can have a negative effect on the service user.

"…two members of [nursing] staff physically held [family member] down …to forcefully give him medication. And [family member] is quite a docile guy…. That was shocking. That actually worsened his condition. He was already bad but that tipped him completely. We were horrified. And I had signed the papers…[for admission]."

Individual variation in the approach of the nursing staff was noted.

"A lot of the staff - the nursing staff - are excellent. Others behave like jailors."

"I had an experience of temporary Inpatient service and… I have the experience of permanent Inpatient service. There is a huge qualitative difference between the two…in that the long-term situation is the build-up of – you know – friendship almost between the patients and the staff…. It's professionalism at its very best. [In short-term stay] they [nursing staff] said to my wife, '[Family member] is treating this place like it is a hotel.' I said, 'He wouldn't be in the place if he wasn't behaving in some unusual way! And I thought their attitude was – I mean they are out of touch with their role."

"….he [family member] was on suicide watch…actually 4 nurses came in and stayed with him. They done shifts but they never got paid for that. They did that themselves!"

The approach of medical personnel was generally experienced as distant and occasionally dismissive. Their reluctance to discuss emerging side effects from medication was of particular concern.

"[Named consultant] was dismissive of anything I would say, even about treatment or facilities…[consultant] was not open about anything."

"…and they [consultants] absolutely refused point blank [to discuss family member issues with the carer]. Medication, stabilisation and you're grand…. No discussion. You're not entertained."

"I had bought the book and read about the thing [tardive dyskinesia] …I went up to the hospital and said 'Look this [treatment side effect] can be irreversible.' First [consultant] said 'Oh no, no.' 'Look', I said, 'it is written down there by a doctor.' And he was taken off it….[medication]."

"Our experience of the hospital was just to give her as much drugs as turns her into a zombie and send her home. And absolutely no co-operation in reducing tablets."

"…there was no structure for the relatives…you had to do it for yourself. And if the first door you push stays closed, you have to have the energy to stay pushing on other doors and find the back door or whatever…"

Some participants dealt with their exclusion from partnership in the care of their family member by creating an alliance with their GP to better manage the medication aspect of treatment.

"Now I have been going on a programme – to give you an example – with [family member] regarding medication…I discovered that he wasn't taking his medication…I said, 'If you don't take these, you're going back into the hospital….' He didn't want to be all his life on this medication. He wanted to be able to control…his thoughts,

which is his right. I could be dead in the morning. I can't be watching whether he's taking his medication or not…. We've an agreement. He came down to [n mgs]…. He's nearly 4 months off medication completely…. Now the GP knows he's off and the consultant says, '… that's why you're well, because you're on the medication" – even though he is not!"

"[Family member] had started to develop this kind of dyskinesia…we went to [consult another doctor] and he advised us to start weaning her off the drug…we did get to 5 mg…had been on 6. And then we noticed that [the] paranoia started coming back so we upped it half-a-milligram for a few months and [service user] was grand…and we put it down half-a-milligram. We stopped going to the clinic because the psychiatrist wouldn't support that. So now we just keep a careful eye on things, ourselves and the GP."

Participants recognised that the physical conditions in many facilities had improved over the years, although the importance of on-going maintenance to keep standards up was also remarked upon.

"[Named location] was a diabolical place. My wife couldn't even go up there. It was just shocking…[like] something out of Dickens."

"Then they refurbished [named location] and I've seen around that and it looked lovely…"

"Three years ago [named facility] had holes in the ceiling, holes in the walls...an unpleasant sort of place to be. I don't know if it's improved any."

However participants expressed surprise that new units could be built without consultation with service users or their carers.

"It is a brand new unit, praised by psychiatrists but built without any consultation with any service user or any relative of service users…"

The absence of access to an open air area, and of easy access to meaningful recreational activities was also an issue. The health risk associated with 'smoking rooms' was noted.

"…denied all access to fresh air. Absolutely no exercise facilities of any sort…to be denied access to fresh air is – I think is probably against the European Convention of Human Rights. Or any form of exercise…and it is a brand new facility! We complained about that [lack of exercise] you know, at length and eventually after a lot of complaining – some of the staff now are brilliant – some of them they brought [family member] out and walked him around the block."

"…they have a games room which consists of a table tennis table to which access is denied unless a member of staff volunteers to play table tennis with them."

"The smoking rooms in there – unbelievable! You don't need to light a cigarette at all like!"

Members of the group felt that insufficient allowance was being made for persons who might need a longer stay in the Inpatient setting.

"[Family member] was in the acute unit for much longer than…the unit is designed to cater for…. There is an assumption that you will be there only for a short time. There is no forward thinking and because of that there wasn't a structure [suitable to a longer stay]."

[Speaking about brief Inpatient stays and the 'revolving door' aspect of the mental health system, a number of participants noted the following]. "They have to get them out of here in a week because the place is too full…. Who are they making room for? Because…we are talking about people [who] are chronic…[who] are legally unwell…they [service users] are coming back in…." [Because of too speedy a discharge on each admission].

Some carers noted that their family member did not feel safe or comfortable in the Inpatient setting.

"…you wake up in the night and an old man looking straight in your face. Or you go to the toilet and come back [and] some old fellow is in your bed or going around in your pyjamas. So if you [are emotionally upset] it is pretty scary."

Topic 4: Day Hospital Service

Carers considered that this service did not exist in fact.

"There isn't any!"

"I asked about a day hospital and I was told that there is no day hospital suitable for your [family member]."

"Well in theory you have day hospitals and day centres scattered through any health board…but they raise issues about how the service users are going to get the places."

"[Family member] attended…a day hospital placement…where he was given 1 hour a week and he was the only person in the class." [There was little opportunity to engage socially with other clients].

Topic 5: Outpatient Service

Participants noted that the discharge process could be quite haphazard and possibly risky for the service user and the family.

"…[family member] just rang and told me that he was sitting down in the foyer. Now luckily he has me and I'm there for him. But the number of people that are discharged and just left back into the community. Nobody checks where they are going to – are they on their own?"

"…they actually left [family member] out after 5 weeks and he was anything but well."

The absence of appropriate 'step down' facilities in some sectors for service users ready to leave the Inpatient setting but not ready to live with their family or independently was a major concern.

"[Because of the effect on other family members] we refused to have him home…. And the resolution was [named hostel] for homeless men was the only accommodation they claimed they could find for him…. He rang me in tears. 'There are people who are alcoholics, there's people who have just come out of jail, criminals. I am afraid in my room.' Like it was absolutely horrific…."

"[There is] no half-way house…."

"It is a matter of where you are. Some sectors [within a health board, and some health boards generally] will be not exactly able to supply, to meet the needs of their [service users]."

"[Some health boards have a policy]…of phased discharge and accommodation provision, but [some] rely on… the city corporation and voluntary bodies…"

"The fact that people can be put out on the street with no plan at all is a scandal…."

The members of this group were very aware of and concerned about the possible plight of service users who had no carer/relative to support them and seek their rights.

"We only got it [after-care services] by fighting for it. I mean friends of friends and people we knew. If he was on his own, he would have nothing at all you know."

"They [service users] can't do anything for themselves. I think they [service providers] should be obliged when they are discharging somebody from hospital – that they should be discharged to an external professional like the psychiatric social person…who can keep an eye on them. Anything else is utterly – it is irresponsible actually."

"And the only people with schizophrenia that avail of these [NTDI and FÁS] courses are people who have carers. The majority of people…they have nobody to – like – [no] outside force to help them along…"

The disengagement of medical personnel from the concerns of carers continued in the Outpatient setting.

"I listed out a whole list of things that I thought [family member] would need and might need. But it was just 'No' to everything. And I said, "So there's nothing so? and I was told "But you have an appointment with Outpatients, haven't you?"

The lack of consultant continuity of care was noted.

"And every single time he goes in it takes 5 minutes [and] it's a different person who reads about him. How can they [monitor service user progress]?"

"…we never saw the same doctor twice!"

"It is humiliating for the patient really. It is, just."

The efficiency of service delivery in Outpatients was commented upon.

"Fifty others [service users] all appear at the same time and you are sitting there waiting, waiting, waiting. Eventually it's a 2 minute job – a jab [injection] and out the door and that's it."

The variation in role of nursing staff between Outpatient settings was noted.

"…the nurse – I mean they should be able to give the injection."

"It was a nurse that gave [service user] the injection."

Carers were generally not informed of the entitlements of their family members or of support services on which they and the service user's family member could draw.

"[GP] took money from her [parent who was a carer in the past] every two weeks when [family member] got his injections…I found out from the community nurse that [caring parent] should not have been paying for it at all…"

"No, there was no information. Only what information, like, [that] all of us here we learned it for ourselves…. When you are caring for the person you learn."

A need for support from community services such as psychiatric social workers, occupational therapists and community officers was expressed.

"Psychiatric social workers…to help you when the person is ill initially. That is the biggest, the hardest time. When you have to take somebody [to hospital] and then the squad car and all that kind of stuff…people don't know what to do or how to approach it or how…. It is getting them help initially."

"And then when they are coming out of hospital again they need daily support and badly need support there again…. Absolutely."

"In our situation [family member] he was getting visits every week or two…occupational therapy for a couple of weeks and the community welfare nurse you know…but once the 6 months was up [this service ended]."

"We never got that [service]."

The rehabilitation service run by NTDI and FÁS was widely praised and the particular suitability of community employment work for service users experiencing schizophrenia was mentioned.

"There's NTDI where you can go through FÁS for courses such as Fresh Start, which is extremely good."

"If somebody goes through that [NTDI] they do their time through FÁS where they go into an employer for a certain length of time. The unfortunate thing is…they are there for 6 months and they are feeling very good about themselves – their self-esteem, their confidence – but the trouble is they only get 6 months, maximum a year."

"Community employment jobs…they are good because they are like short hours and they are very good for people with schizophrenia. But they are very insecure."

Topic 6: Treatment Plan

The group were not aware of any treatment plan as such.

"There isn't anything else other than medication."

"There would be a care plan, but it is all aspirational."

Participants remarked that some boards and sectors did have viable treatment plans.

"Monaghan and Clondalkin? Don't they have plans – they do."

Main concerns of the group

○ Effective system planning is needed. This should include support for early intervention and an adequate and appropriate post-discharge infrastructure (e.g. sheltered accommodation; community based follow-up services etc).

○ Regional bench marking of services and league tables showing the relative quality of the services offered across Boards and across sectors within Boards using objective standards should be introduced.

○ National policy on service user and family/carer rights to be implemented, keeping in mind that some service users may need assistance in activating the policies that apply to them.

O Continuity of care from consultants within the mental health system.

O Policy of medication as the only treatment option should be addressed and other therapies actually made available.

O The ethos should be one of recovery and rehabilitation rather than containment.

O The lines of communication and cooperation between the relevant government Departments of Health and Children; Education; Justice; Social Welfare and Finance should be cleared and made to work efficiently and effectively.

O The following passing remark from a participant at the end of the session struck us as summing up a key concern and anxiety of carers and we propose to include it in our report to the Mental Health Commission -

"Every carer is haunted with the thought 'what happens to the children when the carer dies?' There is nothing for them then."

Appendix V

Technical Note on Establishing Validity in Qualitative

Research Through Triangulation

Validity refers to the extent to which the picture of an issue that emerges from the data as collected and analysed by the researcher concerned gives an accurate understanding of the subject of the research.

When researchers are establishing the validity of their results in qualitative research such as that done here, they will look to see whether their findings are essentially similar in pattern to those found by other researchers working independently. They will be interested to see whether researchers using different methods (e.g., a quantitative as opposed to narrative approach to data collection) will come up with similar findings. They will also examine information from other relevant sources (e.g., accounts by individuals; briefing papers by interested groups of all sorts; policy documents; official reports; even incidents recounted in the media) to see whether the basic themes are the same. Since some of these sources would be operating on a different agenda, they must be used with great caution. Where at least two other checkable and convincing sources provide independent confirmation of the findings of the piece of research in question, all three data sets make up a **triangle** of evidence which suggests that action taken on the basis of the results will be relevant to solving the problem.